CUBE
BOOK

FLOWERS

WHITE STAR PUBLISHERS

EDITED BY

VALERIA MANFERTO DE FABIANIS

text
OVIDIO GUAITA

graphic design
CLARA ZANOTTI

editorial staff
GIADA FRANCIA
GIORGIA RAINERI

translation
CORINNE COLETTE

© 2007 **WHITE STAR S.P.A.**
VIA CANDIDO SASSONE, 22-24
13100 VERCELLI - ITALY
WWW.WHITESTAR.IT

● Blooms of the pink beach of Budelli in Sardinia.

ISBN 978-88-544-0226-3

REPRINTS:
1 2 3 4 5 6   11 10 09 08 07

Printed in Singapore

CONTENTS

FLOWERS

Foreword

Flowers stress the most important stages of our lives. They seal a pact of love and renew it throughout the years. Flowers are a homage to beauty, a sign of esteem and are given to celebrate success and conquest – whether small or large. They make our holidays more joyful, accompany our prayers and strengthen our requests for forgiveness. They welcome new life and accompany the departed. Flowers are constantly present – sometimes they are discreet and almost humble and other times they are proud and sumptuous. They reflect our sentiments and emotional states and are the trusted ambassadors of our thoughts.

Valeria Manferto De Fabianis

Introduction

THE LOVE OF FLOWERS HAS FOLLOWED MAN THROUGHOUT HIS HISTORY. THEIR PERFUME, COLORS AND VELVETY PETALS HAVE ALWAYS BEEN POPULAR WITH PEOPLE OF EVERY RACE AND RELIGION. LOVE OF PLANTS AND THEIR BLOOMS IS A TRULY UNIVERSAL PASSION THAT UNITES PEOPLES INSTEAD OF DIVIDING THEM. AND FLOWERS AREN'T ONLY FOR THE WEALTHY – THEY ENRICH THE LIVES OF RICH AND POOR ALIKE. FIELDS, ROCKY AREAS, DESERTS AND WOODS ARRAY THEMSELVES IN GREENERY AND MULTICOLORED WILD-FLOWERS AND CHANGE THEIR "COSTUMES" ACCORDING TO THE SEASON. MAN'S DESIRE TO DOMINATE NATURE AND TO BEND IT TO HIS WILL HAS RESULTED IN THE CREATION OF NEW FLOWERS. EXISTING SPECIES HAVE BEEN IMPROVED, CREAT-

A lotus flower.

Introduction

ING NEW ONES. FLOWERS HAVE BEEN GIVEN AS GIFTS SINCE ANCIENT TIMES. EGYPTIANS PRESENTED THEIR PHARAOHS WITH FLOWERS; PRIESTS OFFERED FLOWERS TO THE DIVINITIES AND MEN IN LOVE HAVE ALWAYS GIVEN A BOUQUET OF FLOWERS TO THEIR PROMISED BRIDE. THE SIMPLE GIFT OF FLOWERS HAS BECOME CLOAKED WITH VARIOUS MEANINGS ACCORDING TO THE SPECIES OF FLOWERS CHOSEN, AS WELL AS THEIR COLOR, AND THIS HAS RESULTED IN THE GRADUAL DEVELOPMENT OF AN ACTUAL "LANGUAGE" OF FLOWERS. EACH CIVILIZATION AND HISTORICAL PERIOD HAS HAD A DIFFERENT CODE, BECAUSE TASTES AND CUSTOMS CHANGE. WITH THE POPULARITY OF PRESENTING FLOWERS AS GIFTS, A WHOLE NEW ART EVOLVED FOR THE CREATION OF BOUQUETS, GARLANDS, OF-

Introduction

FERINGS, CROWNS, HAIR DECORATIONS AND SO FORTH. FLOWERS ARE ALSO USED TO DECORATE THE HOME AND TO ARRAY WINDOWS, BALCONIES AND FACADES. THE ANCIENT ROMANS PLANTED FLOWERS IN THEIR GARDENS AND IN THE MIDDLE AGES, MONKS AND NUNS ADORNED THE CLOISTERS OF THEIR CONVENTS AND MONASTERIES WITH FLOWERS AND PLANTED HERB AND VEGETABLE GARDENS. GARDENS SAW THEIR GREATEST TRIUMPH WITH THE HUMANISTS DURING THE RENAISSANCE. BOTANICAL GARDENS, TOO, WERE CULTIVATED FOR EXPERIMENTATION AND ACCLIMATIZATION PURPOSES. THE TREND FOR GARDENS FOUND PARTICULAR FAVOR WITH THE CULTURED RULERS OF THE 16TH AND 17TH CENTURIES WHO EXCHANGED NEW PLANTS AND HERBS WITH EACH OTHER.

Introduction

FLOWER MARKETS SELLING PLANTS AND FLOWERS IMPORTED FROM ALL OVER THE WORLD BECAME POPULAR AND THE NUMBER OF COLLECTORS OF FLOWERS AND PLANTS GREW CONSIDERABLY. RARE FLOWERS AND PLANTS WERE PRECIOUS TREASURES THAT TESTIFIED TO THE DEGREE OF CULTURE, KNOWLEDGE AND REFINEMENT OF THEIR OWNERS. THEY WERE A SOURCE OF PRESTIGE AND SOMETHING TO BOAST ABOUT, AND THE GARDENS TO CONTAIN THEM WERE THEIR APOTHEOSIS. FLOWERS HAVE ALWAYS FASCINATED US BECAUSE THEY'RE AN EXPRESSION OF LIFE: FROM THE FLOWER, THE FRUIT, AND FROM THE FRUIT, THE SEED AND A NEW PLANT TO REPEAT THE CYCLE AGAIN AND AGAIN. DECORATIVE FLOWERS, FRUIT-TREE BLOSSOMS, EDIBLE FLOWERS, WILD FLOWERS AND CULTIVATED

Introduction

FLOWERS ALL PARTICIPATE IN THIS EXALTATION OF FORM AND COLOR. FLOWERS ARE INCREDIBLY PHOTOGENIC AND THEY ARE OFTEN THE PROTAGONISTS OF A GREAT VARIETY OF COMPOSITIONS USED IN BOTH RELIGIOUS AND SECULAR FESTIVITIES, WHETHER PUBLIC OR PRIVATE. SOME FLOWER "FANS" ARE CONTENT TO ADMIRE FLOWERS IN THEIR NATURAL ENVIRONMENT, WHILE OTHERS SEE EACH FLOWER AS A SINGLE PIECE OF A MORE COMPLEX MOSAIC IN WHICH FLOWERS AND GREENERY ARE ARRANGED TO CREATE A NEW MASTERPIECE, THE FRUIT OF THE CREATIVITY OF MAN. FASHIONS AND TRENDS CHANGE AND SO DO PREFERENCES FOR TYPES OF FLOWERS. THERE IS ONE FLOWER, HOWEVER, WHICH ENCOUNTERS UNIVERSAL FAVOR: THE ROSE. THIS HAS BEEN ESPECIALLY TRUE

Introduction

SINCE THE 19TH CENTURY WHEN BOTANISTS BEGAN PRODUC-
ING AN INFINITE NUMBER OF ROSE VARIETIES WITH DIFFERENT
SHAPES AND COLORS. THE ROSE HAS CONTINUED TO REAP FA-
VOR YEAR AFTER YEAR. MANY MEANINGS ARE ATTRIBUTED TO
THE ROSE AND IT IS CERTAIN THAT NO FLOWER HAS RECEIVED
GREATER ATTENTION. THE FLOWER COMMUNITY IS ALWAYS IN
FLUX AND NEW SPECIES AND VARIETIES ARE BEING CONSTANT-
LY CREATED, SO WE CAN LOOK FORWARD TO BEING SURPRISED
AGAIN AND AGAIN. NATURE'S PALETTE IS AN INFINITELY RICH
ONE AND HER PRODUCTION IS INEXHAUSTIBLE.

27 ● A carnivorous, red-eyed tree frog awaits his prey on a tropical flower.

28-29 ● The floating market of Srinagar, India.

30-31 ● An elegant formal garden with white roses.

32-33 ● Flowers on a balcony outside Salzburg, Austria.

34-35 ● Bouquets of roses in the Albert Kuyp Market in Amsterdam, Holland.

NATURE IN BLOOM

Flowering White Shasta Daisy (*Crisanthemum maximum*).

INTRODUCTION Nature in Bloom

WE ENJOY GARDENS EVEN IF WE SIMPLY OBSERVE THEIR BEAUTIFUL LAYOUT AND PLANTS FROM A TERRACE OR A GAZEBO. NATURE, HOWEVER, WHEN LEFT IN ITS NATURAL STATE, BECKONS US TO IMMERSE OURSELVES IN HER BOUNTY. A TREE, A POOL OR A GENTLE SLOPE MARKS OUR DIRECTION IN TANGLED PATHS HARD TO MAKE OUT IN THE ABUNDANCE OF GREENERY.

GARDENS, AFTER ALL, ARE SIMPLY THE DOMESTICATION OF WOODS AND FORESTS. AND AS THE TREND TO FENCE IN GARDENS LOST POPULARITY AND THE BOUNDARIES BETWEEN GARDENS AND WOODS DISAPPEARED, NATURE IN ITS WILD STATE MERGED WITH ITS TAMED COMPANION

INTRODUCTION Nature in Bloom

AND WILD FLOWERS WERE MIXED WITH THEIR CULTIVATED COUSINS. THE NEW TREND FOR GARDENS SAW PLANTS AND FLOWERS ARRANGED IN A SEEMINGLY CASUAL AND VAGUELY CHAOTIC WAY WITHOUT ANY LOGIC. BUT EVEN THOUGH NOT APPARENT, THEIR ARRANGEMENT FOLLOWED MASTERFUL DESIGN. EXPERIMENTATION WITH GEOMETRIC ITALIAN-STYLE GARDENS HAD RUN ITS COURSE.

HUMANISTS NO LONGER STROVE TO SHAPE NATU-RE ENTIRELY TO MAN'S DESIRE AND INSTEAD ONLY WANTED TO INTERVENE VERY GENTLY TO MAKE HER MORE WELCOMING TO MAN AND CLOSER TO THE IDYLLIC IMAGE SEEN IN ROMANTIC PAINTINGS.

Nature in Bloom
Introduction

AS GARDENS BECAME CLOSER TO THAT IDEAL, DE-LINEATED FLOWERBEDS DISAPPEARED TO GIVE WAY TO MORE UNOBTRUSIVE AND SEEMINGLY "CA-SUAL" LANDSCAPING WHICH EXPRESSED NATURE IN ITS VERY ESSENCE. GARDENS TOOK ON AN EVER MORE NATURAL AND "WILD" APPEARANCE BUT THE PLANTS INCLUDED AND THEIR POSITIONING WERE THE RESULT OF CAREFUL LANDSCAPING.

IN FACT, IT IS PARTICULARLY IN THE GARDEN WITH WILD FLOWERS THAT NATURE IS EXPRESSED, WITH EVEN GREATER RIGOR BECAUSE SHE IS TRANSPO-SED TO A CIRCUMSCRIBED AREA FOR THE ENJOY-MENT OF VISITORS.

41 • Some pink orchids

42-43 • A field of poppies in the Sibylline Mountains in Umbria.

44 • Chamomile, poppies and other wild flowers.

44-45 • A poppy in a field of lavender.

46-47 ● A field in late spring when all the flowers have bloomed.

48-49 ● An apricot tree in bloom in a yellow field of turnips near Modena in Emilia-Romagna.

50-51 • Hills in Antelope Valley, California.

51 • A field of bluebonnets in Texas.

52-53 • Wild flowers in bloom in
Australia.

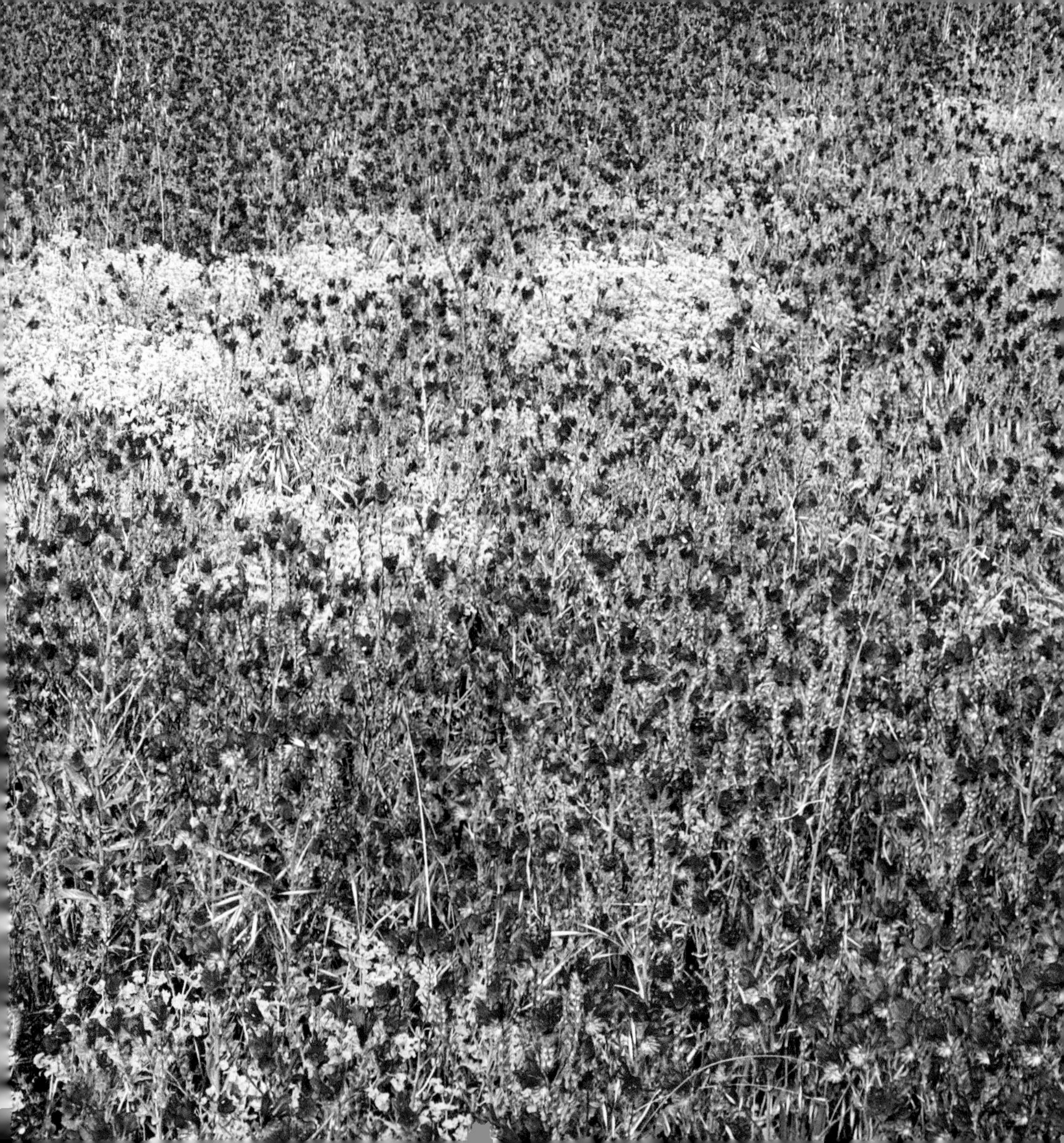

54 • Purple is a color often seen in wild flowers.

55 • A daisy next to a deep purple sage flower.

56-57 • A California Valley with poppies and other wild flowers.

58-59 ● Red poppies cover this valley in California.

60-61 ● The blue, red and yellow "brush-strokes" of wild flowers.

62-63 • A large, purple field in Silverton, Oregon.

63 • Asters in bloom.

64-65 • A field of sunflowers and lupine.

66 • The *Gentiana verna*, a flower which blooms in the Alps right after winter, is very deep blue in color.

67 • A woodland with hyacinths in Surrey, England.

68 ◈ An *Iris marsica* on the Sibillini
Mountains, in Umbria, Italy.

68-69 ◈ Anemones thrive
in the underbrush.

70 • *Soldanella minima* in the Majella National Park, in Abruzzo, Italy.

71 • A natural composition of dwarf cornel and ferns.

72 • Christmas roses in the underbrush of beechwood.

72-73 • A *galanthus nivalis snowdrop* in an Umbrian woods.

74-75 • Crocuses blooming in the woods on Mount Nerone, in Lombardy.

75 • Hellebore in a North American forest.

76-77 • The bright purple of the hepatica beautifully contrasts with the green of the leaves surrounding it.

78 • *Hepatica nobilis*, also known as "Liverleaf", in bloom.

79 • This *geum rivale* has a wool-like stem and a reversed flower.

80-81 • Flowers near a stream in Oregon.

81 • A delicate two-tone orchid in Umbria.

82 • Cyclamens in bloom on a moss-covered fork.

83 • Bluebells blooming in a Northern European garden.

84-85 • The underbrush
of Mount Cucco, in Umbria,
is full of flowers.

85 • Daisies thriving all around
a dead tree trunk.

86 • A field of valeriana tuberosa
on the Sibillini Mountains,
in Umbria.

86-87 • Hundreds of violets
bloom in the shade of the
underbrush.

88 ● Flowers in a valley
at the foot of the Rocky
Mountains, in Canada.

88-89 ● Papaveraceous flowers
are striking when seen against the
snow in Alberta, Canada.

90 • Spring flowers at the foot of Monte Raiser, Washington.

91 • Multicolored lupines blossom throughout New England.

● A hill full of *Lilium alpinum* in the Sibillini Mountains, in Umbria.

94 • In the heart of summer, a bush of edelweiss in bloom in the Abruzzo Apennines.

95 • Its soft, felt-like petals make the Edelweiss unmistakable.

96 • Some *Campanula alpestris* peek out from a heap of stones in the Sibillini Mountains, in Umbria.

96-97 • Flowers along a stream in the Pyrenees in Spain.

Crocuses blooming on the Gran Sasso, in Abruzzo.

100 • Two Eryngium alpinum or "queen of the Alps."

101 • The "queen of the Alps", the *Eryngium alpinum*,
has characteristic star-shaped leaves.

102 • Two *Cistus salviaefolius* near
Lago Trasimeno, in Umbria

102-103 • The *Cistus incanus* (red rock
rose) is a typical Mediterranean flower
which blooms profusely though its
corollas wilt after just one day.

A small, purple flower peeks out of a dense bush of needles.

106-107 • An orchidea sambucina in bloom in Gran Sasso, Abruzzo.

107 • An aconite or *Eranthis hyemalis* which bloomed while the snow was melting on Gran Sasso, in Abruzzo.

108 • The *Pulsatilla vernalis* blooms between April and June at high altitude.

109 • A hellebore, with its characteristic green petals, hides in the snow of the Alps

110-111 ● An thriving expanse of hortensia in view of the Green Lagoon and the Blue Lagoon on the Island of Sao Miguel, in the Azores. Unfortunately, this plant which was imported from Asia, is invasive and threatens the local ecosystem.

112-113 ● Typical Mediterranean vegetation in Porto Greco, Sardinia.

114-115 ● Wild flowers on the Sardinian coast.

● Helicrisum flowers thrive on the Island of Capraia, off the coast of Tuscany.

118 and 118-119 • Dense and splendid expanses of greenery in bloom along the coast of the island of Budelli, in Sardinia.

120-121 • A field of flowers on the Isola dei Gabbiani (Island of Seagulls), in Sardinia.

122-123 • *Abronia villosa* in Joshua Tree National Park, in California.

Abronia villosa and *Oenothera deltoides* in Joshua Tree National Park, in California.

126 • Cactuses blooming in the Nevada mountains.

127 • A view of cactus in Organ Pipe National Park, in Arizona

● Cactus *(Opuntia basilaris)* flowers in Arizona: 'rough' plants like the cactus produce incredibly delicate flowers.

130 • The dwarf prickly pear is present in many Mediterranean regions.

131 • Thousands of escolzia flowers blooming on the arid soil of Organ Pipe National Park, in Arizona.

132-133 • Purple flowers amongst the thorns of a cactus.

134-135 • Cholla flowers, or *Opuntia bigelowi*, blooming in the Sonora desert in Arizona.

136 • A striking array of cactus blooms in Capitol Reef National Park, in Utah.

137 • A natural composition of red corollas and yellow pistils amongst the thorns of a cactus.

138 • The Saguaro cactus blooms between May and June in the southern part of the United States.

139 • Flowers amongst the thorns of a cholla cactus in the Anza-Borrego desert, in California.

140 • A cactus in Spring bloom in a desert area of Utah.

140-141 • The characteristic yellow flowers of the *barrel cactus*.

142-143 ● Large water lilies cover the surface of this lake in Pantanal, Brazil.

143 ● A lotus flower in bloom displays the delicate pale pink to white shading of its magnificent petals.

144 • In the archipelago of Guadalupe, and throughout the Caribbean region, alamanda flowers grow spontaneously.

145 • Frangipane flowers, with their waxy and fragrant surface, are a common sight in tropical regions.

146 • The *Rafflesia arnoldii*, discovered in 1818 on the Island of Sumatra in Indonesia, has the largest flower in the world which has a diameter of more than a meter.

147 • Tropical orchids are the most beautiful representatives of this complex and numerous plant family.

- A solitary lily amongst wild greenery.

150 • An orchid with wine-red petals.

151 • An *Ophrys apifera*, a beautiful orchid with purple petals.

- Flowers in shades of red are the most striking and they attract the most insects and pollinator birds.

● Appearances can be deceiving: the ripe fruit of a Madagascar Tambourissa, an angiosperm, looks like a flower.

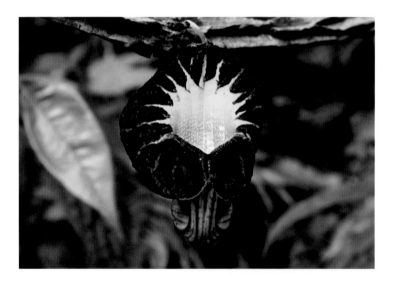

156 • An aristolochia in the Henry Pittier National Park, in Venezuela.

157 • Known as the *"ginger red torch"*, this flaming aristolochiacea blooms on the Caribbean island of Trinidad.

158 • In the shade of the forest, fiery clivia flowers are striking against the dark green of the leaves.

159 • A royal protea, the *Protea cynaroides*, in Maui, Hawaii.

160 • Petals and radiating pistils give perfect symmetry to the *Passiflora amethystina*.

161 • A splendid hybrid of the Louisiana iris grown in South Africa.

Two *Eucalyptus nutans* flowers on the coast of western Australia.

164 • A *cattleya triana* orchid in Costa Rica, where its endemic.

165 • Spontaneous frangipani blooms in the Seychelles.

166 • In the archipelago of Guadalupe, Marie Galante Island is famous for its flowers, many of which grow spontaneously.

167 • A purple orchid in Malaysia where an very wide variety of orchids grow spontaneously or are cultivated in greenhouses.

168 • A beautiful pink and white orchid in Sri Lanka.

169 • The *Passiflora edulis* is also known as the "passion flower".

COLORFUL
SCENERY

• A field of multicolored tulips in the Dutch countryside.

INTRODUCTION Colorful Scenery

GARDENS ARE SMALL MICROCOSMS COMPRISED OF A COLLECTION OF DOMESTICATED NATURAL PLANTS. THEY WOULD HAVE GROWN TO DIFFERENT SHAPES OR IN DIFFERENT SOIL BUT, THROUGH THE EFFORTS OF MAN, THEY ARE TRAINED TO WITHSTAND THE CLIMATES AND TO THRIVE IN THE AMBIENCES HE DESIRES. GREENHOUSES ARE ADDITIONS TO GARDENS WHICH TAKE "ARTIFICIAL" NATURE TO ITS EXTREME. IN THEM, EXOTIC PLANTS, OUT-OF-SEASON FLOWERS AND PLANTINGS THRIVE, AND THE PROFUSION OF GREENERY THEY CONTAIN IS THE OBJECT OF MUCH ADMIRATION. TODAY, THE NUMBER OF GARDEN AFICIONADOS IS STEADILY INCREASING ALONG WITH FLOWER SHOWS. BUT GARDENING IS AN ANCIENT PASSION; IN 1574, ALFONSO D'ESTE, DUKE OF FERRARA, WROTE A LETTER TO MEHEMET PACHA ASKING HIM FOR "FLOWER SEEDS ... TO

INTRODUCTION Colorful Scenery

PLANT IN MY GARDENS". IT WAS THROUGH THESE PIONEERING GARDENERS THAT MANY PLANTS – INCLUDING THE LILAC, HIBISCUS AND TULIP – REACHED THE WEST. THE NEED TO CLASSIFY PLANTS IN A SCIENTIFIC WAY LED TO HERBAL GARDENS (*GIARDINI DEI SEMPLICI*) AND MANY TREATISES WERE WRITTEN TO CATALOGUE THE BOTANICAL KNOWLEDGE OF THAT TIME. PLANTS WERE CLASSIFIED WITH INSTRUCTIONS FOR THEIR CARE, BUT THESE BOOKS MOSTLY GAVE ADVICE ABOUT THE ARRANGEMENTS OF GARDENS ON THE BASIS OF THEIR RELATED SYMBOLISM. THE FIRST BOTANICAL GARDEN IN EUROPE WAS PLANTED IN PADUA IN 1545 BY ORDER OF THE SENATE OF THE SERENISSIMA REPUBLIC OF VENICE (THE CHIEF IMPORTER OF PLANTS FROM THE ORIENT). IN 1591 THE FLOWERBEDS OF THESE HIGHLY COMPLEX GARDENS HELD 1168 DIFFERENT HERBS AND PLANTS.

Colorful Scenery
Introduction

A FEW YEARS EARLIER, *THE HERBALL OR GENERALL HISTORY OF PLANTES* BY JOHN GERARD, WAS PUBLISHED IN ENGLAND. THIS WAS THE CORNERSTONE OF EUROPEAN GARDENS AND HELD THE SUM OF 16TH CENTURY BOTANICAL KNOWLEDGE. WITH THE BUILDING OF THE CRYSTAL PALACE FOR THE GREAT EXHIBITION HELD IN LONDON'S HYDE PARK IN 1851, "ARTIFICIAL" NATURE WAS AWARDED ITS TEMPLE AND SINCE THAT TIME, HAS ATTRACTED MANY FOLLOWERS. FLOWERS AND DOMESTICATED PLANTS HAVE ENTERED ALL HOMES, AND THEY DECORATE BALCONIES AND TERRACES EVERYWHERE. GARDENING IS AN UNIVERSAL PASSION THAT BREAKS THROUGH ALL BARRIERS OF IDEOLOGY AND CLASS – AND HAS VERY FEW OPPONENTS! NATURE BELONGS TO US ALL, EVEN "ARTIFICIAL" NATURE!

● A funny-looking scarecrow guards a field of sunflowers.

176-177 ● A composition of dahlias in their most popular hues.

177 ● Shades of red and purple and bright yellow pistils: Nature teaches us a great deal about the art of arranging flowers.

178 • A group of red azaleas, a very popular flower in Europe and America.

179 • *Cluster amaryllis*, a small bush with a great number of flowers.

Primroses (left) and greenhouse
hyacinths (right).

182 • An aquilegia or columbine is also called "perfect love" or "hidden love".

183 • A purple *Gloxinia*.

A striking color combination: yellow sunflowers on a carpet of purple flowers.

190-191 and 192-193 •
From pale pink to bright
red: nature seems to
blush before such
beauty.

194-195 ● The chastity of white imposes itself on the passion of red in Lisse, Holland.

196-197 ● A field of multicolored tulips in a farm in Mossy Rock in Washington.

198 • Tulips with fully opened petals keep company with hyacinths in the gardens of Keukenhof in Amsterdam.

199 • Red tulips in a field of hyacinths.

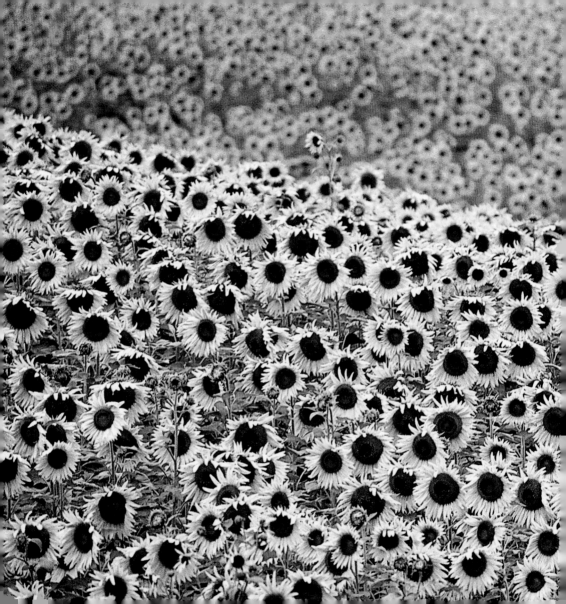

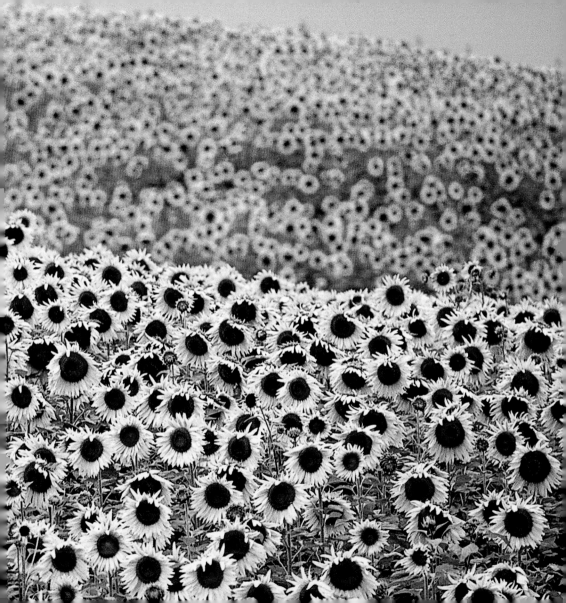

206-207 • Stones placed in a long row mark the path to the sea in this field of rapeseed in Holland.

207 • Yellow is protagonist in this field in Edna Valley, California.

208-209 • Yellow and red tulips.

210-211 • Wide and narrow rows in a great variety of colors are seen in this California nursery.

212-213 • Lavender marks
the borders of a field of grain.

214-215 and 215 • Expanses
of lavender on the hills
in Provence, France.

216-217 • A solitary windmill
dominates this field of tulips in
the Dutch countryside.

● Iris flowers in an Oregon nursery.

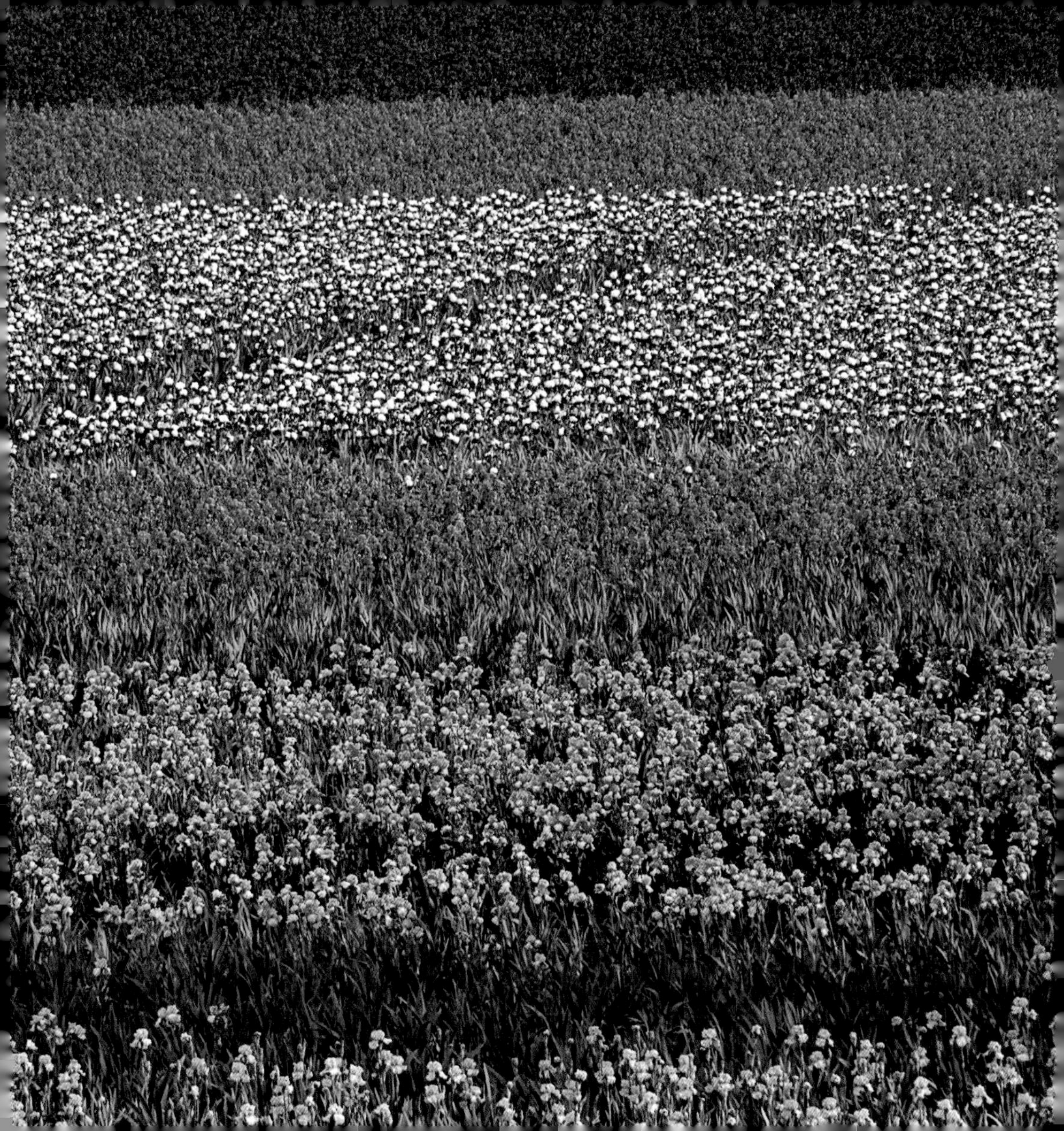

• Various species of *Clarkia* in bloom in late Spring.

222 • The bud of a sunflower before it opens.

223 • Sunflowers in full bloom.

A funny scarecrow on a bicycle guards this field of sunflowers.

A mosaic of plants and greenhouses in Japan.

Bhutan farmers cross a field of canola, from which an oil is extracted, and buckwheat.

230-231 • A field of lotuses near Kampong Chhnang, in Cambodia.

231 • An expanse of pink lotuses.

AT THE FLOWERS WINDOW

Flowers on a balcony on the Island of Panarea in Italy.

INTRODUCTION Flowers at the Window

Windows and balconies are sources of light and air. They look out to the world but they're also filters between two separate worlds, the public one of the streets and piazzas and the world inside which is private and sacred. They make tangible man's need to meet his fellows and to explore his surroundings. Balconies and windows mediate between public and private while at the same time safeguarding the privacy of the home. They are both for protection and participation, because while they are screens defending us, they also permit observation, display and interaction with the outside. Throughout the Orient and in the Islamic countries, there are very few windows looking out to the street, and when they exist at all, they are very nar-

INTRODUCTION Flowers at the Window

ROW AND HIDDEN BEHIND GRATING OR PERSIAN BLINDS. THIS PREVENTS THE WOMEN OF THE HOUSE FROM BEING OBSERVED FROM THE OUTSIDE. IN THE WEST, INSTEAD, WINDOWS ARE FEATURED AND DECORATED. WHETHER ONLY AN OPENING OR AN ACTUAL ELEMENT OF DECOR, WINDOWS ARE AN IMPORTANT PART OF THE FACADE AND ARE OFTEN DECORATED WITH WINDOW BOXES FILLED WITH FLOWERS. WINDOW BOXES AND BALCONIES ARE GARDEN SURROGATES AND WHILE LANDSCAPED GARDENS ARE THE PREROGATIVE OF THE WEALTHY, IT IS WITHIN MOST EVERYONE'S REACH TO GIVE FREE REIN TO THEIR CREATIVITY BY COMBINING THE PLANTS THEY PREFER AND ROTATING THEM ACCORDING TO SEASON. BESIDES THE CULTURE OF A CIVILIZATION, CLIMATE, THE AMOUNT OF SUNLIGHT, TECHNOLOGIES AND MATERIALS HAVE ALWAYS INFLUENCED HOW WIN-

Flowers at the Window

DOWS AND BALCONIES ARE ARRAYED WITH FLOWERS AND PLANTS. BUT WINDOWS AND BALCONIES ARE BASICALLY ONLY "SPACES" AND THEIR CHARACTER IS PROVIDED SOLELY BY THEIR POSITION, FORM AND DECORATION. FLOWERS AND PLANTS DECORATE AND COLOR THEM WHILE ALSO SCREENING THEM AND MAKING THEM LIVELIER AT THE SAME TIME. GOD ADVISED NOAH TO CREATE AN OPENING IN HIS ARK FOR THE DEPARTURE OF THE DOVE OF HOPE AND THE BIBLE TELLS US THAT SOLOMON'S TEMPLE HAD LARGE WINDOWS, WIDE TOWARDS THE INTERIOR AND NARROW TOWARDS THE EXTERIOR. THE HISTORY OF WINDOWS IS A LONG AND STATELY ONE. WINDOWS ARE AN ESSENTIAL ELEMENT OF ARCHITECTURE, AND MAN'S PASSION FOR FLOWERS AND PLANTS MAKES THEM MORE BEAUTIFUL.

Geraniums in bloom on a balcony at the foot of Mount Civetta, in Veneto, Italy.

238 and 238-239 • Traditional homes in Switzerland (left) and in Germany are made livelier with flowers.

240-241 • Cascades of geraniums, pelargoniums and fuchsia almost hide this rural home in southern Germany.

242-243 • An old Lazio
home with a balcony full of
red and pink geraniums.

243 • Flowers on a balcony
in Marostica, in Veneto, Italy.

244 • Flowers on a balcony in the spa city of Bath, England.

245 • This façade of a Roman house is almost completely covered with flowers.

246-247 • A example of a botanical collection in Cordoba, Spain.

248 • The elegant French colonial
architecture of the Royal Cafe in
New Orleans, Louisiana.

248-249 • Pots of surfinia petunias
make a balcony in New Orleans
more beautiful.

• Flowers make any building more beautiful. Here, we see a bare wall with a pot of flowers ingeniously inserted in it (left). Note the striking contrast offered by the ivy and ornamental flowers.

252-253 ● A cascade
of flowers and plants
on a balcony in the
historical center of
Anguillara, in Lazio, Italy.

254-255 ● A triumph
of flowery decoration
near Salzburg, Austria.

23
Dorfheimerstraße

A façade multicolored with flowers in Cantabria, Spain.

258 • These hibiscus plants in bloom lean away from the terrace in search of sunlight.

259 • A unique contrast between static strength and transient beauty: a masculine statue supports a balcony in the center of Genoa, Italy.

• A historical building
in dell'Oberbayern,
Germany with religious
frescoes and flowers
at the windows.

Cascades and galleries of flowers exalt the welcoming Mediterranean atmosphere of a town in Grand Canary, Spain.

An accordion player
practices among the
surfinia petunias and
the geraniums.

266 • Bougainvillea beautifully insinuates wherever it is planted. Here, we see
a flowery façade in Mentone, France.

267 • The celebrated sunshine of southern Europe – here, the South of Spain –
wouldn't be as attractive without spectacular balconies full of flowers like these.

268-269 • In Cartagena, Columbia, brightly colored facades reflect the colors of the flowers of the loggias.

270-271 • The Swedish candor of this building make the flowers on the balcony of a Sunne cottage even more striking!

272-273 • Sunflowers make a splendid still life whatever the container and wherever they are.

274 • Whether terracotta or wood, the container doesn't matter:
what attracts attention are the flowers!

275 • A pot of *wisteria* and *kerria* elegantly peek from this window.

276-277 ● A "hanging garden" in Rome's Piazza Navona.

277 ● A "hanging garden" in Rome's Piazza Navona.

278-279 ● Flowery 'screens' – in this case, petunias, garden balsam and lobelia – provide protection from indiscrete onlookers.

Signs and historic buildings are decorated with geraniums creating a timeless view of the towns in Baviera, Germany.

282-283 • Cascades of flowers with various bicycles leaning against a wall in Dinkelsbühl, Baviera.

284-285 • A corner window in Allgäu, Baviera, with Spring flowers.

OUR FRIENDS IN NATURE

A green hummingbird in the forests of Costa Rica.

INTRODUCTION Our Friends in Nature

THE MYTH OF EDEN WAS GRADUALLY REPLACED WITH THE MYTH OF ARCADIA, THE CLASSICAL TALE BY VIRGIL THAT WAS REDISCOVERED DURING THE RENAISSANCE. AT FIRST, IT WAS ONLY A LITERARY TREND, BUT IN THE LATE 17TH CENTURY IT SPREAD TO THE VISUAL ARTS, MUCH TO THE DELIGHT OF LANDSCAPE DESIGNERS. THEY BECAME ENAMORED WITH THIS SORT OF SECULAR PARADISE, WITH ITS GROTTOS, RUINS AND TEMPLES PEOPLED BY SHEPHERDS PLAYING THE FLUTE AND BY SATYRS AND NYMPHS WHOSE LORD WAS CLOVEN-FOOT PAN. THE FAUNA WAS OF SCIENTIFIC INTEREST, AND ADMIRED FOR ITS BEAUTY, BUT ANIMALS WERE ALSO THE PREY OF ENDLESS HUNTS IN THE WOODS AND FORESTS MUCH LOVED BY THE NOBLES OF THAT PERIOD. THESE AREAS, THOUGH SHAPED

INTRODUCTION Our Friends in Nature

BY MAN, WERE IN PERFECT HARMONY WITH THE NATURAL WOODLANDS. THEY WERE AN ELABORATE ORNAMENT TO THE ACTUAL GARDEN AND WERE ALSO THE PRECURSORS OF THE ROMANTIC PARKS OF THE 18TH AND 19TH CENTURIES. BEYOND THEIR MACROSCOPIC PRESENCE, HOWEVER, CLOSE-UPS OF THE FLOWERS AND SHRUBS SHOW A FANTASTIC MICROCOSM WHERE NATURE REIGNS IN ALL HER CHAOTIC ORDER. HER PLAYERS INCLUDE THE MANY TYPES OF INSECTS THAT POPULATE FLOWERS, PLANTS AND THE UNDERBRUSH. THESE UNSUNG HEROES GUARANTEE THEIR CONTINUITY AND – THROUGH A COMPLEX HIERARCHICAL SYSTEM – ALSO ASSURE THE EQUILIBRIUM OF THE SPECIES. WHILE WE DELIGHT IN THE BEAUTY OF THESE DELICATE ECO-SYSTEMS, THOUSANDS OF TINY

Our Friends in Nature
Introduction

CREATURES ARE BUSY WORKING TO MAINTAIN IT BY BAT-
TLING THE HOSTILE INVADERS WHICH FROM TIME TO TIME
TI IREATEN TO DISTURB ITS BALANCE. IT IS A TRUE ARCADIA
BUT MUCH MORE BRUTAL THAN THE ONE DESCRIBED BY
VIRGIL – AND MUCH MORE INTRIGUING!

THIS FANTASTIC WORLD, HOWEVER, IS ONLY VISIBLE USING
MACRO PHOTOGRAPHY OR PATIENTLY OBSERVING IT
THROUGH A STRONG MAGNIFYING GLASS. THIS EXCITING
LIVING MICROCOSM TAKES OUR BREATH AWAY, AND
OUR SENSE OF DISCOVERY GRADUALLY GIVES WAY TO
WONDER, ALL GENERATED BY THIS VARIED AND OFTEN BI-
ZARRE ENVIRONMENT THAT TRULY EXPRESSES THE IDEA
OF ARCADIA.

- An African frog on a flower in Akagera National Park, in Rwanda.

292 • Tiny hummingbirds help flowers in an important way: when they feed on the nectar
of a flower, they collect pollen which they deposit on the next flower they visit, fertilizing it.

293 • A hummingbird feeds on a "fire ginger" in Costa Rica.

294 • Nectar is the most important element in the diet of hummingbirds and tropical flowers are particularly juicy and rich in nutrients.

295 • A hummingbird feeding on a *Cavendishia bracteata*.

296 • A yellow-breasted canary upside-down looking for nectar.

297 • A wren hunting insects on the stem of an umbrelliferae .

298 • A moth flying next to a *Silene dioica*.

299 • A moth in search of nectar on a *Lonicera periclymenum*.

300 • The flowers to provide the *Junonia Orithya* of Malaysia nourishment are in the background. Its pretty dappled wings don't camouflage it; their orange spots defend it from predators because they look like fierce eyes.

301 • A *Melanargia Galathea* with black and white wings on a centaurea scabbiosa.

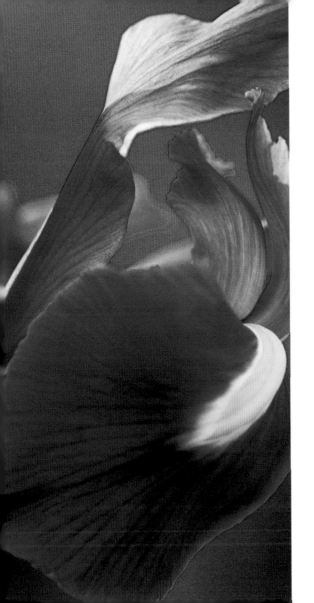

302-303 • Light, dappled wings
against a bright purple iris.

303 • A butterfly sucking
in the nectar of an aster.

303

304 • Of all the "baits" used by flowers to attract insects and thereby perpetuate their species, color is the most important one.

305 • A butterfly balanced on the pistil of a flower.

306 • A male *Anthocharis cardamines* on an alcanna (henna) plant.

307 • A *Lysandra bellargus* on a *Pulicarya dysenterica* flower.

308 • The beauty of the Inachis is striking against the daisies in the background.

309 • A butterfly on a clump of purple daisies.

310-311 • A dragonfly flying low over the water ready to land on a water lily.

312 • Its need for nectar was fatal to this bee captured by a crab spider.

313 • A leaping spider jumps on a sirfide fly just as it lands on a flower.

314 • A moth getting nourishment from buddleia flowers.

315 • A bumblebee exits a *Geum rivale* after having fed on its nectar.

316 • A large dahlia welcomes the bumblebee which has dived into its pollen.

317 • A pollen-covered bee on a *Verbesina alternifolia*.

318-319 • A queen bumblebee flying towards the flowers of a *Ribes sanguineum*.

319 • A honey bee landing on a flower.

320 • Even though its pollen sacks are full, it still visits a consolida maggiore (comfrey).

320-321 • Using its proboscis, a bumblebee punctures the base of the corolla of a comfrey flower.

● A *Micropteropus pusillus* bat heads for a Kigelia pinnata flower also known as a "sausage tree". To the contrary of what is believed, not all bats are insect eaters. Some, like the *pusillus*, get their nourishment from fruit, pollen and seeds.

324 • A fly stretches out its proboscis towards the stamen (male organ of flowers) of a *Rhingia campestris.*

325 • A beetle in search of food; the majority of these insects eat vegetables and devour flowers from root to petals.

● Gold beetles (here photographed on a wild carrot flower, left, and on a red thistle, right) eat greens but they are so rare nowadays as to no longer pose a threat to agriculture.

• A *Cernuella virgata* snail and *Papilio rutulus* caterpillar: both snails and caterpillars often eat flowers and plants and are enemies of gardens and fields.

Ladybugs (here, on a marsh marigold, left, and a primrose, right) are friends of flower gardens because they eat the aphids which cause great damage.

● Ladybugs climbing on flowers in search of prey. Only one sub-family of this species eats greens and is damaging to gardens.

Stretched out to drink from this flower, this ladybug quenches its thirst from a drop of water.

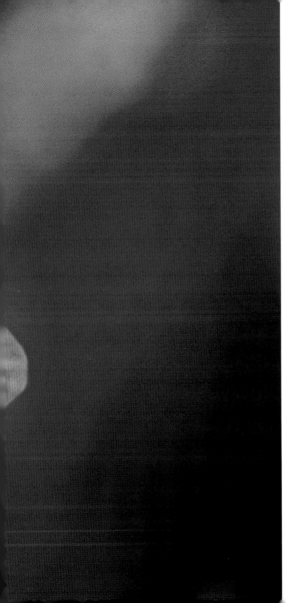

● Locusts (left) and grasshoppers (right) do the most damage to plants and flowers.

• The fleshy flowers of Costa Rica attract two bizarre grasshoppers for different reasons: the *Copiphora rhinoceros*, left, is looking mainly for greens while the *Lirometopum coronatum*, right, is probably hunting a prey.

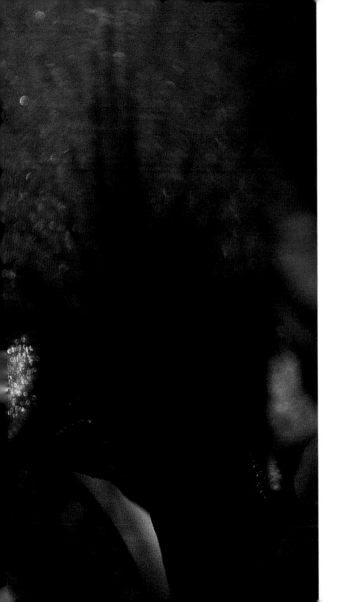

A grasshopper in its kingdom among the succulent petals, pollen and leaves which are its food and which provide a good place to lay eggs.

● To the contrary of grasshoppers, the *Pseudocreboter whalbergi* mantis of Tanzania, left, and the *Choerododis sp.* , right, on a bougainvillea flower, are both carnivores and use flowers only to ambush their prey.

344-345 • A snail in search of food bends the stem of a *Chrisantemum maximum.*

346-347 • A domestic spider explores an expanse of corollas in search of prey.

Experts at camouflage, the crab spider is also known as the "flower spider" because it usually hides in ambush in flowers.

A green spider (left) stands out against the colorful flowers while the crab spider does all he can to become invisible, though it might take him several days to take on the color necessary for camouflage.

Almost one with the strelizia, a Jackson chameleon prepares to capture a prey.

354 • An Arizona alligator lizard *(Elgaria kingii nobilis)* waits for his meal to walk by on the white petals of a calla lily

355 • A felsuma (of the gecko family) stands watch from the top of a Nile lily. This small animal eats both nectar and insects.

356 • An Imantodes inornatus, twisted around a Heisteria branch shows why its popularly called the "tree snake" as it lies in ambush in a tree.

357 • A deadly *Bothriechis schlegeli* viper explores an eliconia flower.

● Red-eyed tree frogs *(Agalychnis callidryas)* peeking out of an eliconia, left, and a "fire-ginger flower", right.

● Hunting prey, the White frog *(Litoria caerulea)*, left, in on an eliconia, and a red-eyed tree frog, right, is taking advantage of the flowers of the tropical forest to search for prey, especially in the bag of the *Paphiopedilum orchid*, right, which is a trap for insects..

Strong tropical flowers like the bromeliacee offer ideal "launching pads" to hunting frogs, Here, we see two red-eyed tree frogs.

The batracian, the poisonous *Dendrobates pumilio* ("branch climber", left) and the *red-eyed tree frog*, right, show their absolute dependency on tropical flora.

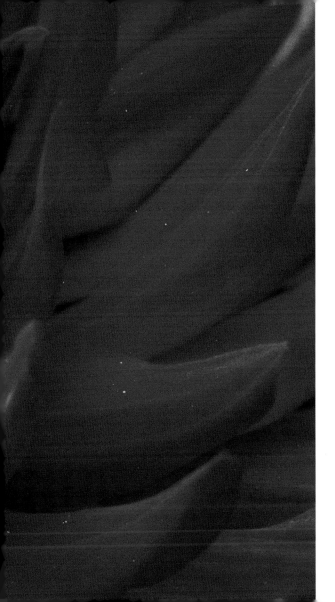

Even though its ambush station is bizarre, this tree spider seems to feel at ease in this dahlia.

A WORLD OF ROSES

• The corolla of a red rose creates a vortex around the invisible anthers containing the pollen.

A World of Roses
Introduction

WHEN HOLLAND DISCOVERED A PASSION FOR TULIPS, WHICH AT THAT TIME WERE CONSIDERED EXOTIC, IN THE BEGINNING OF THE 17TH CENTURY, EVERYONE WITH A GARDEN WANTED TO GROW THEM. IN THE GOLDEN AGE OF THE DUTCH BOURGEOISIE, COMPANIES WERE FOUNDED TO EXPLOIT THE NEW FLOWER COMMERCIALLY IN ALL ITS COLORS. LATER, IN THE 19TH CENTURY, THE CAMELLIA WAS ALL THE RAGE AND BECAME THE QUEEN OF EUROPEAN GARDENS WITH ITS ALMOST 200 VARIETIES. THE CAMELLIA ORIGINATED FROM THE ORIENT (KOREA, CHINA AND JAPAN) AND IT WAS FIRST IMPORTED TO EUROPE TO BE USED AS A TEA. SOON, HOWEVER, BOTANISTS AND COLLECTORS BECAME FASCINATED WITH THE BEAUTY OF ITS SPLENDID FLOWERS.

- The popular tea rose blooms between June and October.

INTRODUCTION A World of Roses

THE ROSE, HOWEVER, ONLY BECAME POPULAR IN EUROPE IN THE 19TH CENTURY EVEN THOUGH IT WAS MENTIONED BY THE EGYPTIANS – AND SUBSEQUENTLY, THE GREEKS AND ROMANS – MUCH EARLIER. IN THESE CULTURES, ROSES WERE USED FOR ORNAMENTAL PURPOSES AND FOR THE EXTRACTION OF ESSENTIAL OILS FOR COSMETICS. ONCE THEY BECAME POPULAR IN EUROPE, HOWEVER, THE PASSION FOR ROSES KNEW NO BOUNDS AND HAS NOT YET ENDED.

IN THE FIRST HALF OF THE 19TH CENTURY, ROSES WERE PLACED IN FORMAL ROSE GARDENS BUT LATER, THEY WERE POSITIONED IN AN APPARENTLY CASUAL MANNER IN ROMANTIC GARDENS.

AFTER THE PUBLICATION OF THE BOOK *LES ROSES*, BY THE BELGIAN PAINTER PIERRE-JOSEPH REDOUTÉ (CALLED "THE RAPHÄEL OF FLOWERS") IN 1824, ROSES BECAME EVEN MO-

INTRODUCTION A World of Roses

RE POPULAR. THE BOOK WAS A FANTASTIC ANTHOLOGY OF ROSES, AND INCLUDED PAINTINGS OF 170 ROSES, RENDERED WITH THE REFINEMENT OF A ROMANTIC ARTIST AND WITH SCIENTIFIC AND BOTANICAL RIGOR AS WELL. NUMEROUS OTHER PUBLICATIONS ABOUT ROSES FOLLOWED, KEEPING THE ROSE IN ITS GLORIFIED POSITION. WHETHER ITS REIGN WAS DUE TO ITS ANCIENT ALLUREMENT OR TO ITS WEALTH OF SYMBOLIC AND HISTORICAL CONTENT – ACCORDING TO MYTHOLOGY, VENUS GAVE THE ROSE ITS BEAUTY AND DIONYSUS GAVE IT ITS HEADY FRAGRANCE – IT BECAME (AS THE GREEK POETESS SAPPHO REFERRED TO IT LONG AGO) THE "QUEEN OF FLOWERS."

INDEED, CLEOPATRA HAD WELCOMED ANTHONY WITH A CARPET OF ROSES; JULIUS CAESAR OFTEN WORE A ROSE CROWN; BOTH NERO AND POPPEA SPENT HUGE AMOUNTS

A World of Roses

Introduction

OF MONEY TO SURROUND THEMSELVES WITH ROSES; AND JOSEPHINE BONAPARTE HAD THE MOST FAMOUS ROSE GARDEN OF HER TIME. TODAY, ROSES HAVE A PLACE IN EVERY GARDEN, ESPECIALLY IN TEMPERATE CLIMATES. ROSES PREFER SOIL WITH A HIGH CLAY CONTENT, THEY DON'T LIKE TO SHARE THEIR SPACE WITH OTHER PLANTS AND THEY NEED TO BE TRIMMED YEARLY.

THERE ARE 107 ROSE GENRES AND MORE THAN 3000 DIFFERENT SPECIES, INCLUDING WILD ONES AND EDIBLE ROSES, WHICH BELONG TO THE SAME FAMILY EVEN THOUGH THEIR FLOWER LOOKS DIFFERENT.

AND PERHAPS, MOST IMPORTANT OF ALL ARE RED ROSES WITH THEIR VELVETY PETALS AND INEBRIATING PERFUME, AND WHICH SYMBOLIZE LOVE.

- An arch of roses welcomes visitors to a Welsh cottage in Wales, Great Britain.

A classical rose garden with the traditional pastel colors of temperate climates.

This incredibly bright rose was named for John Clare (1793-1864), the most important English naturalist poet.

This bud trying to get through the opened corollas reflects the most ancient symbolism connected to the rose: rebirth.

The rose is probably the most difficult flower to describe. As Gertrude Stein wrote: "A rose is a rose is a rose and as we see from these two bouquets of English roses.

● The Felicia rose is
particularly delicate and
doesn't like pruning.

386 • It's natural for roses to be often named for poets and writers: this spectacular hybrid, for example, is dedicated to William Shakespeare.

387 • A salmon colored English rose which is a very widespread type in Europe.

388-389 ● English roses are characterized by cup-shaped corollas and have numerous petals.

389 ● A rose which has just bloomed.

390 ● The roses created by botanist, David Austin resemble the so-called "ancient roses" but have a much wider range of colors.

390-391 ● Roses are also ideal for rustic bouquets.

392 • Some Charmian roses.

392-393 • A composition of English roses in full bloom.

394-395 ● The thin petals
of this English rose allow
its stamen to be seen.

395 ● English roses are a cross
between ancient roses and
Tea roses.

● Protagonists in the historical ambiences which suit them very well, *Scepter'd* Isle and *Snow Goose* (left) and other English roses (right) seem to shine in the shadow.

398 • Beautiful in its simplicity, the *Rugosa alba* rose with its thick petals is very strong and not difficult to grow.

399 • The yellow Happy Child roses, which are very common in Europe, boast the brightest yellow of all English roses.

Delicate White Wing roses are characterized by their visible anthers, and with warm colored Golden Celebration roses they make an ideal composition.

A touch of refinement: the shower of Goldfinch anthers with their white petals give warmth to the generous Felicia rose.

In these pictures, taken by a famous botanical photographer specialized in portraits of roses, these compositions of roses seem to have been painted by an Italian 17th century master artist.

- The corollas of many
botanical roses,
close enough to the
reproductive organs
of the rose to hide
them, may have
even 100 petals.

The variety of species (about 25,000 species of garden roses created up to now) offer infinite composition possibilities as shown by this still life of red English roses, berries and apples, left, and by the pretty picture on the right.

• Clair Matin roses, created in 1960, are resistant to drought and cold and are perfect when used as large hedges.

412 • Timeless roses are well named for the pleasure they give observers.

413 • Yellow roses symbolically refer to joy, promise and memory ...but to jealousy, too!

● The herbs and background flowers are important elements of rose compositions in vases. On the left, we see the airy erba stella with an achillea on the right to support the magnificent beauty of the roses.

416 • Cup shaped flowers, not very big but perfectly shaped are a characteristic of the
English heritage roses created in 1984.

417 • Gratitude (bright pink), admiration (pastel pink) and desire (coral) could
be the sentiments expressed in rose "language" of this composition.

● "Hybridization" is usually a term with negative connotations but it is only thanks to this process that we are able to enjoy an infinite variety of roses.

• Red roses are the most
sensual ones and their
symbolic meaning is
naturally "passion".

An enchanting view of Portloe, England (left), and a more modest one of Grand Coteau, Louisiana (right): whether expertly cared for or not, roses always create unique and unrepeatable beauty.

- The colors of roses, besides their symbolism, are related to their strength. Generally, coral and ornage roses are less resistant than dark red ones.

426 • White roses in bloom in
a garden in Tampere, in Finland.

426-427 • A formal garden in Alderney
Grange, in the Channel Islands.

● Roses are also distinguished on the basis
of their number of petals: simple (less than
8), semi-double (8 or more), double (more
than 20) and très-double (more than 40).

430-431 • A beautiful English Heritage rose in the *Ausblush* variety.

431 • English *Crocus Roses* in the *Ausquest* variety.

432 • The English *Scepter'd Isle* rose, introduced in 1997, blooms from June to September.

433 • The *Octavia Hill* rose, created in 1993, blooms repeatedly throughout the warm season.

A rose arbor and the famous blue sky of British Columbia, Canada, create an atmosphere in Butchart Gardens which isn't very northern-like.

Rose bushes in Sweden (left) and on the Island of Nantucket, in Massachusetts (right): throughout the world, roses in gardens, which are usually the hardy rose bush type, are placed against fences to make them more beautiful and to make them stronger.

438 • Climbing roses do much to make old and neglected facades more beautiful.

439 • A rose bush embellishes a corner of a traditional home in Gerberoy,
in northern France.

440 • *Countryman* roses are very hardy and the bloom continuously even in winter if temperatures don't drop below 8°C-9°C.

441 • *Wise Portia* roses have characteristic points on their petals.

A rustic wall in Sauternes, in eastern France, becomes a thing of beauty because of this climbing rose.

444 • This English Tea rose has a pretty feminine name: *Emily*.

445 • Introduced in 1949, the Aloha rose blooms from early summer to early autumn.

446 • The *Bonica* rose is a hardy rambling rose and is ideal for the covering of low walls and rocks.

447 • The "Singin'in the Rain" rose, in line with its name, doesn't like dry climates and blooms in the rainy season from early spring to early summer.

The high decoration potential of roses is due to their many varieties. Roses can be bushy, climbing, rambling, tree-like or cascading.

450 • The *Countryman* rose bush has characteristic "flat" flowers with a wealth of petals.

451 • Leaves, in terms of color and thickness, are another distinguishing characteristic of roses. Some roses have leaves which are deep green and very thick.

Climbing roses in Stockbridge, England, and in Siasconset, on the Island of Nantucket, in Massachusetts.

454 • This white rose in the sunshine of an Italian garden has only been in bloom for a couple of days.

454-455 • The *Bonica* rose is identified by its unique color: it appears to be blushing

Yellow climbing roses in Obidos, Portugal, warm the cold sky of this Atlantic country.

458 • *Brandy* roses, introduced in 1981, are derived from Tea roses
and have large flowers with a unique and elegant shape.

459 • Its pure color identifies the *Graham Thomas* rose which is considered
to be the most beautiful yellow rose of all the modern English roses.

❀ The beauty of a cottage in the United Kingdom owes much to roses. Here, we see two facades: in Cotswolds, England (left), and in Stradbally, Ireland (right).

462 and 462-463 •
Roses in Göteborg, Sweden (left),
and on a ruin in Cernika, Slovenia
(right), because of their great
ornamental value do much to make
wherever they are planted more
beautiful and lively.

464-465 • Climbing roses are
used to decorate walls and to
create rose arbors like this one
in the United States.

466-467 • *Rosa mundi* is one of the most ancient garden roses and possibly dates back to the 15th century.

467 • The hardy, two-tone *Oranges 'n' Lemons* rose doesn't fear a chilly climate.

468-469 • White roses of the island of Madeira, in Portugal: this Atlantic island is the site of an important flower festival.

470-471 • Leonardo da Vinci and Degenhard roses produce a great number of blooms.

472 • Since the time of the caliphs in Spain, roses have embellished the Generalife gardens, in Granada.

472-473 • Climbing roses at the entrance of the Rose Garden of the master botanist, David Austin, in England.

474 • The color of pink-apricot yellow is typical of Tea roses.

474-475 • One of the most popular white roses is the *Iceberg* rose which blooms until early winter.

In August, English gardens are in full bloom and are at the height of their splendor.

● *Climber* roses (left) bloom repeatedly in summer and produce large flowers. *Rambler* roses (right), instead, bloom only once and have small, cascading flowers.

480 • *Chinatown* roses in bloom near banksia and clematis flowers in Gunby Hall, England.

480-481 • Roses in bloom on arches and fences create a spectacular path in Granada, Spain.

482-483 • The natural elegance and luminosity of a solitary rose seen in Butchart Gardens in Brentwood Bay, Canada.

FESTIVE FLOWERS

A little girl, wearing a crown of flowers, takes part in a mid-summer festival in Skepparkroken, Sweden.

INTRODUCTION Festive Flowers

Gardens, plants and flowers frequently complement celebrations. This relationship is widespread, and it's connected to traditions that are often ancient and strongly rooted in the cultures of many peoples. The baroque garden made a great contribution to western garden design and was the sovereign stage for memorable parties held amidst an array of flowers, labyrinths made of shrubs and green theaters with the seats and stage made of boxwood. Other outdoor theaters included the so-called "water theaters" comprised of basins of water and lively wa-

INTRODUCTION Festive Flowers

TER SPOUTS IN AN AREA SURROUNDED BY ROCKS AND "FLOWER THEATERS" WITH SPLENDID FLORAL COMPOSITIONS IN VASES DECORATING SQUARES, STAIRWAYS AND PATHS. FLOWERS ARE AN ESSENTIAL PART OF THE MAJORITY OF OPEN-AIR EVENTS WHETHER JOYFUL OR SAD, PRIVATE OR PUBLIC, ANCIENT OR CONTEMPORARY AND THIS IS TRUE THE WORLD OVER.

FLOWERS ARE NOT ONLY ASSOCIATED WITH THE GRANDIOSE ARISTOCRATIC PARTIES HELD IN THE GARDENS OF THE NOBLES, BUT ARE ALSO TRADITIONALLY ASSOCIATED WITH A NUMBER OF CELEBRATIONS AND ARE AN IMPORTANT PART OF MANY RELIGIOUS AND POPULAR HOLIDAYS TH-

Festive Flowers
Introduction

ROUGHOUT THE WORLD. SOMETIMES, FLOWERS ARE JUST A PART OF THE STAGE, BUT OFTEN BOUQUETS OF FLOWERS CLOTHE DANCERS AND PRIESTS OR ARE WOVEN INTO GARLANDS, CUSHIONS, CARPETS OR WALLS. YOUNG GIRLS CROWNED IN FLOWERS ANNOUNCE THE COMING OF SPRING AND, IN HAWAII, VISITORS ARE WELCOMED WITH FLOWER NECKLACES. IN TIBET, MONKS CREATE MULTICOLORED CARPETS MADE OF FLOWERS DURING THEIR RELIGIOUS CELEBRATIONS WHILE IN THAILAND, THERE'S A SMALL TEMPLE FOR FLOWER OFFERINGS TO THE DEITY FOR PROTECTION IN FRONT OF EVERY HOME.

- Fragrant tropical flowers are arranged in a traditional composition for this flower festival in Chiang Mai, Thailand.

490 • Young brides in India are getting ready for a group marriage ceremony
with flowers in their hair and colorful flower garlands.

491 • A statue of the monkey god, Hanuman, covered in an abundance of flowers
in a procession in Puttaparthi, India.

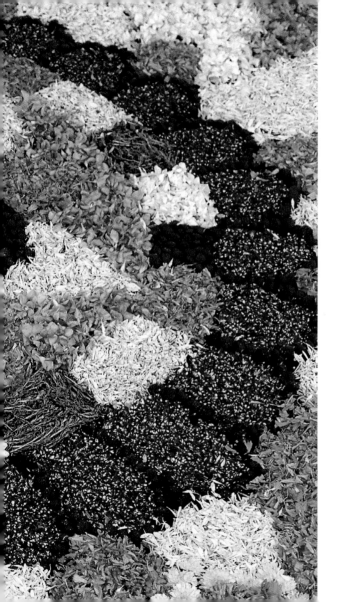

A traditional *pookalam* composition is ready for the *onam* harvest festival in India.

Flowers are sold to be used as offerings in front of the Dargah Mosque in Ajmer, India.

● In Pushkar, India, offerings of flowers are very often given to honor a *shivling* which
is the sacred phallus of the supreme god, Shiva (left), and to decorate the head of Nandin,
the bull (right) his mythological steed.

In Sravanabelgola, India, two Jain monks arrange the *kalasa* (bowls of flowers) for a celebratory *mandala*.

Dressed like royalty with flowers in their hair, adolescents take part
in a ceremony to ordain novice monks (the *Poy Sang Long*)
in Mae Hong Son, Thailand.

● The mother of a
novice proudly carries
an elaborate flower
offering during the Poy
Sang Long ceremony,
in Thailand.

504-505 and 506-507

● Thousands of leaf "boats", carrying candles and flowers, are placed in the water during the Loy Kratong festival, a thanksgiving festival for the fertile waters, in Thailand.

● Portrayals of mythological beings and divinities made of flowers are taken on parade during the flower festival in Chiang Mai, in northern Thailand.

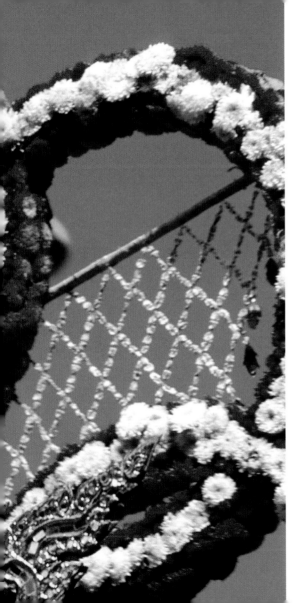

The flower festival is held yearly
at the end the cool season (in February)
to celebrate the wealth of flowers
in the region.

Decorated with images of the Buddha, a cart in the flower festival portrays a complete Buddhist temple group.

514 • A group of Chinese children are waiting to take part in the parade for the Chinese New Year in Chinatown, in Vancouver, Canada.

515 • The colorful traditional costumes of southern China (here, in the region Guilin) often include flowery headdresses.

A cart in the style of the Chinese opera, is on parade in Pasadena, California, during the Tournament of Roses, a popular flower parade established in 1890.

Carts from the Edo period (1603-1867), re-painted and adorned with floral decorations, are on parade during the Chichibu festival, in Japan, which has been held for the past 300 years.

Flowers have a place of honor in a number of Japanese festivals: left, we see a child taking part in the Gion festival, in Kyoto and to the right, we see a little girl parading in the Arashiyana festival which celebrates the arrival of autumn.

● The Hakata Dontaku festival in Fukuoka, Japan, uses new blooms for the ladies' hair decorations.

- Apprentice Balinese dancers
wear headdresses comprised
of very fragrant flower
compositions

• Necklaces and ornaments of flowers and grasses are worn by the participants in the festival held in the Island of Yap, in Micronesia which includes a dance competition among the villages.

528 ● The beautiful and abundant nature in the Island of Samoa is reflected in the many varieties of flowers used for the characteristic flower necklaces popular throughout Oceania.

529 ● A little girl dressed in a hula costume carries a basket filled with Hawaiian lei, the well-known necklaces made of frangipani flowers which are popular in Hawaii.

530 • Frangipani flowers worn by a young *hula* dancer.

531 • Fragrant frangipani flowers *(Plumeria)* are worn by this child sounding
a shell during a festival in the Cook Islands.

The rules of the Rose Parade in Pasadena, California, are clear: the carts to participate must be decorated using only materials from the vegetable kingdom: petals, seeds and various types of bark.

In Medellin, the "city of flowers" in Columbia, the local florists parade through the streets every year carrying their most beautiful compositions on their backs.

536 • Sometimes, the weight of a composition presented in the Medellin festival (even 70 kilograms) is more than the weight of the florist to carry it.

537 • About 500 florists take part in the Medellin festival which was established one hundred years ago.

538 • In the city of Villa Franca do Lome, in the Azores, a rose festival is held every year with a parade of carts.

539 • In Madeira, Portugal, a famous flower festival is held in April to celebrate the return of Spring.

• During the Romeria del Rocio, in Spain, a procession of carts decorated with baroque flower compositions are heading for the Santuario de la Paloma Blanca en Almonte.

● The cart most laden with flowers during the Romeria del Rocio procession is naturally the one carrying the statue of the Virgin Mary to whom the pilgrimage is consecrated.

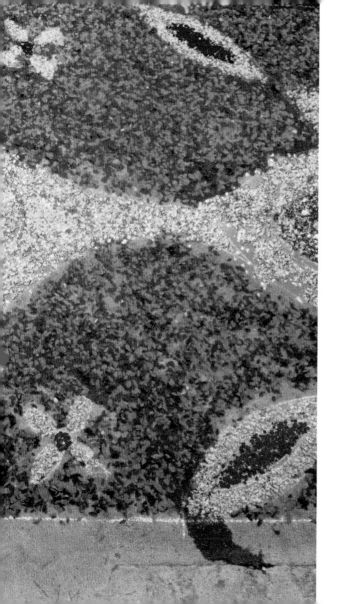

During the flower festival in Costa Brava, Spain, street artists create a large "painting" using the petals of a variety of flowers.

Carnival, in sunny Nice, France, includes a parade of carts decorated with an abundance of flowers.

548 • A very young lady portrays Spring in this festival in Stiria, Austria dedicated to the arrival of the warm season.

549 • A child in costume holds a bouquet during the Nice carnival. It is believed that the Nice carnival was used as the model for the Rio carnival in the late 19th century.

The narcissus festival sees boats laden with narcissus flowers,- used to portray a variety of characters and decorations - parade on Grundl Lake in Stiria, Austria every year to celebrate the abundance of this flower in the area.

The parade of "cows" in the tulip festival in Woodburn, Oregon.

The Grand Place di
Bruxelles, in Belgium,
hosts a flower show
every year which
covers the center of
town with blooms.

556 • A cart of beer barrels, decorated with flowers and leaves, on its way to the Baviera statue in Monaco di Baviera, Germany.

557 • Flower decorations on a cart highlight the lively atmosphere which pervades the Oktoberfest beer festival in Monaco di Baviera.

558 • A dancer performing the Morris Dance, a popular English folk dance, is wearing a hat with striking flower decorations.

559 • In perfect Druid style, a young lady crowned with flowers is taking part in the National Eisteddfod of Wales, in Great Britain.

The ancient religious tradition of the *infiorata* (flower 'carpeting') to celebrate Corpus Domini in Italy (left, Genzano, Lazio; right, Spello, Umbria) through the centuries has become a true form of art with the creation of masterpieces made of flowers.

562 ● In Bolsena, Lazio, in Italy, a mosaic of flower petals pay homage to the celebrated Cherubs by Rafael.

563 ● This classical composition of flowers was made for the *infiorata* to celebrate Corpus Domini in Bolsena, Lazio.

564-565 ● Artists at work preparing the *infiorata* in Genzano, Lazio.

FLOWER MARKETS

• A young person offering a plate full of flowers Bharat, India.

INTRODUCTION Flower Markets

Whether for the public at large or only for wholesalers, flower markets are magical places. The mixture of fragrances fills the air, and the colors, voices and people create a fairy-tale atmosphere. The odors are different from the synthetic perfumes created by industry and express the true fragrant essence of the earth. Whether flowers are grouped in bouquets of single bright colors or combined to create impressionist masterpieces with every hue of the artist's palette, the individual flowers are the stars of the flower markets, which can be floating ones on boats or can be set up in city squares with a myriad of stalls. In Asia, flowers are often sold by men and women squat-

TING, THEIR HEADS HIDDEN UNDER BIZARRE CONE-SHAPED STRAW HATS. BUT, HOWEVER FLOWERS ARE SOLD, THEY ALWAYS ATTRACT BUYERS AND ADMIRERS. WE ARE UNDER THE MAGICAL SPELL OF FLOWERS EVEN IF WE DON'T KNOW THEIR BOTANICAL NAMES. JUST SEEING A GREAT MANY FLOWERS IN THE SAME PLACE PUTS US IN A GOOD MOOD AND THIS IS TRUE EVERYWHERE. THEIR PRECIOUS PETALS MAKE STREETS AND PIAZZAS MORE BEAUTIFUL AND EN-CHANT EXPERT GARDENERS AND PASSERS-BY ALIKE. EVEN IN THE POOREST AND MOST ISOLATED REGIONS OF OUR PLANET, FLOWERS ARE GIVEN AS PRESENTS. THOUGH THE MEANINGS ASSOCIATED WITH THIS CUSTOM CHANGE AND THE TYPES OF FLOWERS VARY ACCORDING TO CLIMATE AND TERRAIN, THIS WONDERFUL PRODUCT OF NATURE IS

Flower Markets

Introduction

APPRECIATED ALL OVER THE WORLD. FLOWERS CAN BE BEST ADMIRED IN MARKETS WHERE THEIR COLORS AND VARIETIES CAN BE COMPARED AND THEIR FRAGRANCE CAN BE ENJOYED TO THE FULLEST… AND WE CAN PURCHASE THEM AND MAKE THEM OUR OWN. FLOWERS GIVE US A SWEET DOSE OF SERENITY, ESPECIALLY WHEN THEY ARE A PART OF OUR EVERYDAY ENVIRONMENT. WE MUSTN'T FORGET THAT FLOWERS ARE ALSO USEFUL IN THE KITCHEN AND NOT ONLY THE FRIED SQUASH FLOWERS THAT EUROPEANS LOVE. ROSE PETALS ARE AN INGREDIENT IN MANY TYPES OF ICE CREAM, WHILE SALADS OF FLOWERS, A FAVORITE IN THE ORIENT, ARE NOW SERVED THROUGHOUT THE WORLD, ESPECIALLY ON THE TABLES OF HEALTHY CUISINE.

A flower market in Amsterdam, Holland, the land of tulips.

572-573 • A flower-seller
in Rajasthan, India.

573 • In India, it is customary
to sell flowers with their stems
cut off at the corolla.

574 ● Baskets of flowers in a market in Rajasthan, India.

574-575 ● The flowers sold in India are usually used for the altars to make offerings to the divinities.

576-577 ● A seller of flower garlands at work in a market in Bangalore, India.

578 ● Sellers of flower garlands in Kolkata (Calcutta), India.

579 ● The flower market in Varanasi (Benares), India.

A florist is the Victoria Park flower market, in Hong Kong, arranged blooming plum branches, believed to bring good luck, for the Chinese New Year celebration.

582-583 • Bouquets in Thailand (here, seen in the Bangrak market, in Bangkok) are usually wrapped in banana leaves.

583 • Flowers to be used for compositions, instead, are wrapped in newspapers.

A seller of roses is arranging her wares in a flower market in Bangkok, Thailand.

586 • Flowers and vegetables are mixed together in this market in Pai, Thailand.

586-587 • Flowers in Thailand are sold in huge quantities and are used mainly for religious offerings.

Lotus flowers are especially popular in Thailand and are sold with their blooms still closed (left) and when they are just about to open (right).

In Thailand, flower garlands like these are used exclusively for devotional purposes and are unscented.

592 ● A flower-seller going to market
in Da Nang, Vietnam carrying his
traditional baskets..

592-593 ● Flower-sellers in the central
market in Can Tho, Vietnam.

594 ● A flower-peddler offering
her merchandise in Taunggyi,
Myanmar.

594-595 ● A florist arranges
bouquets to be used as offerings
in Yangon, Myanmar.

Burmese flower-sellers: left, an elderly woman in the capital city, Yangon and right, a women in the port city of Thantwe.

598 ● A flower seller from the northern part of the country goes to the market in Kalaw, Myanmar.

598-599 ● Peddlers of flowers and vegetables exchange their merchandise in the floating market on Lake Inle, in Myanmar.

● Tulips and sunflowers are for sale in the market in Singel, Amsterdam,
Europe's flower capital.

602-603 ● Amsterdam isn't the only Dutch city to give space to flowers: here, we see the Blumenmarkt ("flower market") in Delft.

604-605 ● This photograph depicting the lively flower trade in Holland was taken in Amsterdam.

Large, white calla lilies steal the scene in this Funchai market, on Madeira, the Portuguese island which boasts an extraordinary wealth of flowers.

• The flower market in Stuttgart, Germany covers the whole square.

610 • A colorful stall selling carnations in the Moore Street market in Dublino, Ireland.

611 • Sunflowers for sale in the Columbia Road flower market, in London, England.

612-613 • In a street market in Stockholm, Sweden, bouquets of flower are in bags ready to be sold.

613 • Tulips for sale in Stockholm's Norrmalmstorg Square.

614 • A flower stall in via Croce, Rome.

615 • A flower market held in Piazza Anfiteatro ("Amphitheater")in Lucca, Italy.

616-617 and 617 • In the romantic city of Paris, it's common to find many large and small open-air flower markets.

618-619 • Yellow and pink chrysanthemums are simply and effectively arranged according to color.

A wealth of flowers animate the historical center of Aix-en-Provence, France. All of Provence and the bordering Leghorn Riviera are famous for their magnificent cultivated flowers.

622 • Shopping for sunflowers
and carnations in Coustellet, in
Provence, France.

622-623 • Cassis lavender in
Provence: these fragrant flowers
are king in the flower kingdom.

624-625 • Open-air markets in Boulevard Edgar Quinet, Paris.

625 • Bouquets of hyacinths in the Faubourg St. Germain market in Paris.

626-627 • The flower market in Grand Place of Brussels in Belgium.

628-629 • An eye-attracting display: chrysanthemums and gerbera in a variety of colors arranged for sale.

630-631 • The flower market offers various hybrid flowers including these unusually colored chrysanthemums.

632 • A flower-seller awaits customers in the Friday market in Antananarivo, Madagascar.

633 • In a Cape Town market, a woman sells Protea flowers. These flowers date back 300 million years and they are characteristic of South Africa.

634-635 • Sunflowers and lilies for sale in Seattle, Washington.

635 • A florist proudly displays her Oriental-type flower arrangement on a Seattle street.

636 ● The florists' market in Dallas, Texas.

636-637 ● A display of dahlias in Seattle's Pike Place Market.

638-639 • The Atwater Flower Market in Montreal, Canada.

639 • A stall of sunflowers in an open-air market in San Francisco, California.

640-641 • Bolivian women sitting on the ground selling flowers in the Ciudad Punata market.

642 and 643 • Women in Guatamala selling flowers and wood for burning
in the Sunday market in Chichicastenango.

644-645 • Aided by her daughters, a women prepares bouquets of flowers
on a street in Quito, Ecuador.

646 • A flower-seller wearing a characteristic "work hat" selling lilies at the Cuenca market, in Ecuador.

647 • A little Indio girl selling calla lilies at the Chichicastenango market, in Guatemala.

SAY IT WITH FLOWERS

- A heart made of flowers sends a clear message.

INTRODUCTION Say it with Flowers

IN THE ORIENT, THE TULIP SYMBOLIZES PERFECT LOVE, WHILE IN THE WEST IT MEANS FICKLENESS. THIS IS JUST ONE EXAMPLE OF THE LANGUAGE OF FLOWERS, WHICH, NEEDLESS TO SAY, CHANGES FROM PLACE TO PLACE AND CULTURE TO CULTURE. IN THE MIDDLE AGES, WHEN A YOUNG LADY GAVE A KNIGHT TWO DAISIES TO DECORATE HIS SHIELD, IT WAS A PUBLIC DECLARATION OF LOVE WHILE, IN OTHER ERAS, LADIES WORE A DAISY CIRCLET ON THEIR FOREHEADS TO SHOW THAT THEY WERE UNSURE OF THEIR LOVERS. ONE AMERICAN INDIAN CUSTOM WAS FOR A YOUNG MAN TO GIVE HIS CHOSEN LADY A BRANCH OF MIMOSA, AND IN THE LAST CENTURY IN ENGLAND, GIRLS WORE A SPRIG OF MIMO-

INTRODUCTION Say it with Flowers

SA IN THEIR HAIR TO TESTIFY TO THEIR FEMINIST IDEO-
LOGY – A CUSTOM THAT IS STILL IN PLACE TODAY. SAINT
JOSEPH IS OFTEN REPRESENTED WITH A STAFF IN HIS
HAND, A LILY BLOOMING AT ITS TIP TO SYMBOLIZE PU-
RITY AND CHASTITY. ACCORDING TO THE GREEKS, THE
LILY ORIGINATED FROM A DROP OF MILK THAT SPILLED
FROM JUNO'S BREAST AS SHE WAS BREAST-FEEDING
HERCULES.

SOMETIMES, THE MEANINGS OF FLOWERS ARE THE SA-
ME IN DIFFERENT CULTURES. ORANGE BLOSSOMS, FOR
EXAMPLE, WERE USED DURING THE CRUSADES TO DE-
CORATE WEDDING GOWNS, AND FOR THE ENEMY SARA-
CENS, THEY HAD ALMOST THE SAME MEANING: FECUN-

INTRODUCTION Say it with Flowers

DITY. RED ROSES, TOO, HAVE A UNIVERSAL MEANING: LOVE AND PASSION. ROSES OF OTHER COLORS HAVE MEANINGS ACCORDING TO THEIR HUE: YELLOW FOR JEALOUSY AND INFIDELITY, WHITE FOR PURITY AND CHASTITY AND PINK FOR CHARM AND SWEETNESS. THE RED CARNATION ALSO EXPRESSES LOVE AND PASSION; THE WHITE ONE MEANS FAITHFULNESS. IN SPAIN, JASMINE IS THE EMBLEM OF SENSUALITY AND IN TUSCANY IT IS ADDED TO BRIDAL BOUQUETS EVEN TODAY. PEONIES ARE TO BE PRESENTED TO A SHY AND BASHFUL LADY LOVE WHILE IN CHINA AND JAPAN PEONIES WERE THE FLOWERS OF EMPERORS, WHO WERE THE ONLY ONES PERMITTED TO PICK THEM. PETUNIAS, BECAUSE THEY

INTRODUCTION Say it with Flowers

BLOOM INCESSANTLY AND PROFUSELY, SYMBOLIZE WILD AND UNCONTROLLABLE PASSION. THE NARCISSUS OWES ITS FAME TO OVID'S METAMORPHOSIS, WHICH TELLS OF A HANDSOME SHEPHERD WHO FALLS IN LOVE WITH HIS OWN REFLECTION IN THE WATER. THE VIOLET EXPRESSES MODESTY AND SHYNESS BUT ALSO VANITY AND AN INCAPACITY TO FALL IN LOVE WHILE THE PRIM-ROSE SYMBOLIZES YOUTH AND PRECOCITY, BECAUSE IT IS THE FIRST TO BLOOM IN SPRING.

FLOWERS, HOWEVER, SOMETIMES HAVE NEGATIVE MEANINGS. YELLOW CARNATIONS SYMBOLIZE SCORN, AND CYCLAMEN IS THE SYMBOL OF MISTRUST, BECAU-SE ITS ROOTS ARE POISONOUS. LAVENDER HAS THE SA-

Say it with Flowers

Introduction

ME MEANING BECAUSE OF THE MANY HORNETS AND BEES ATTRACTED TO IT WHEN IT IS IN BLOOM.

IN HAWAII, WOMEN WELCOME VISITORS BY PLACING A GARLAND OF FLOWERS AROUND THEIR NECKS. ALL OVER THE WORLD, BRIDES FOLLOW THE TRADITION OF TOSSING THEIR BRIDAL BOUQUETS TO THEIR UNMARRIED GIRLFRIENDS. *IKEBANA*, THE ART OF "LIVING FLOWERS," A HISTORICAL FLOWER-ARRANGING TECHNIQUE THAT BEGAN IN ABOUT THE 6TH CENTURY, IS STILL VERY POPULAR TODAY ESPECIALLY IN JAPAN. FLOWERS ARE THE GRAMMAR OF A UNIVERSAL LANGUAGE AND ONE OF THE FEW TRULY UNIVERSAL IDIOMS.

• A bouquet of roses is ideal for a bride because its meanings are "desire" (peach-colored roses), "unity and faithfulness" (white roses) and "happiness in the home" (yellow roses).

656 • Mimosa, which we see peeking out of this bouquet, stands for "women's' determination".

657 • IPansies, depending on type, mean either "capriciousness" or "forgiveness".

● Neutral containers are generally used for flower compositions in order to not distract from the effect created or from the message implied.

Rustic containers are striking when holding bouquets comprised of a variety of flowers (left) and or even just modest wild flowers (right).

662 • Wedding bouquets where antique pink is the predominant color are very refined and stand for "perfect happiness".

663 • When a knight gave his lady a bouquet of daisies in the Middle Ages, it was a public declaration of love.

A side-by-side comparison: a sensually refined composition on the left and a modest bouquet on the right.

666 • A vase to be used a a centerpiece for a special occasion.

667 • The austerity of the container used highlights the romantic and somewhat decadent character of this centerpiece.

668 • The presentation of a garland of multicolored flowers
is a gesture of welcome in many countries.

669 • A composition of daisies, carnations and other flowers,
with their different meanings, is an ideal gift.

670 • A centerpiece of roses is perfect even in a very elegant setting.

671 • An elaborate centerpiece of white roses, symbol of purity, celebrates the bride.

672, 673 and 674-675 • Whether real (left) or made of sugar (right), especially when combined with orange blossoms (next page), roses express many meanings linked to marriage including pure love, grace, hope and innocence.

FRAGRANT
PALETTES

- Light shading accompanies the crinkling of these rose petals.

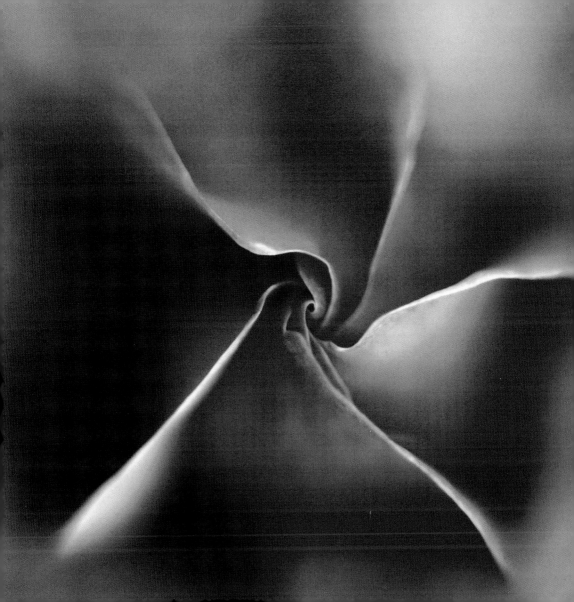

INTRODUCTION Fragrant Palettes

Perfumed and with velvety, multicolored petals, flowers have always captured man's attention. The wide variety of shapes and colors has always unleashed the imagination of composers, painters and photographers. Flowers are like the instruments in an orchestra – each has its own special role in creating the symphony that accompanies human life. They soothe, calm, alert and inebriate us with their magnificence and punctuate our history and beliefs. It is even told that carnations bloomed from Mary's tears as she wept at the foot of the cross.

Modern technology has opened up a whole new world of possibilities for flower lovers. The pho-

INTRODUCTION Fragrant Palettes

TOGRAPHER CAN TAKE CLOSE-UPS THAT WOULD HAVE BEEN UNTHINKABLE EVEN JUST A FEW YEARS AGO AND OUR MODERN CHEMICAL AND DIGITAL "CANVASES" PERMIT THE PHOTOGRAPHER EXCITING, NEW CHROMATIC AND FORMAL POSSIBILITIES OFTEN CLEARLY REMINISCENT OF THE WORK OF MIRÓ, KANDINSKY AND, ESPECIALLY, MONDRIAN, WHO WITH HIS UNCONTAMINATED FIELDS OF PURE COLOR SEEMS TO HAVE BEEN THE INSPIRATIONS FOR THE PHOTOS THAT FOLLOW. NATURE, HERE, BECOMES A CO-STAR AS PHOTO-GRAPHY MEDIATES REALITY, MUCH LIKE RENAISSANCE GAR-DENERS DOMESTICATED IT BY OBLIGING IT TO BEND TO MAN'S DESIGN. LEAVES, STEMS, PETALS, PISTILS, POLLEN, AS WELL AS ENTIRE FLOWERS ARE MORPHED BY THE CLOSE-UP LENS AND TAKE ON AN ABSTRACT, OUT-OF-CONTEXT

Fragrant Palettes
Introduction

AND EMPHASIZED APPEARANCE WHERE THE MYRIAD SHA-
DES OF GREEN ARE ONLY A SMALL PORTION OF THE COLORS
COMPRISING THE PHOTOGRAPHER'S PALETTE.

WONDERS OF NATURE THAT SHE HIDES FROM THE HUMAN
EYE AND REVEALS ONLY TO POLLINATING INSECTS ARE EX-
PLORED IN THIS CHAPTER SHOWING US THE DETAILS COM-
PRISING THE FLOWER'S INTIMATE ESSENCE. THE PHOTO-
GRAPHER'S INDISCREET LENS EXPLORES EVERY PRIVATE
CORNER OF THE FLOWER AND, BY WORKING WITH LIGHT LIKE
A MODERN-DAY IMPRESSIONIST, THE HEIRS OF MONET SHA-
PE OUTER REALITY TO INNER VISION AND INTIMATE UN-
DERLYING DEPTHS FOR THE DELIGHT OF OUR READERS.

686 • Raindrops on a blue iris.

687 • The blue and white petals of the *Aquilegia vulgaris*.

688 • A dahlia opens its heart to the first rays of the sun.

689 • The pistils of a camellia.

690-691 • Not silk drapes moved by the wind, but rather dahlia petals.

691 • An burst of yellow on an iris.

692-693 • A flaming Penelope dahlia.

694 • Almost like a wheel with numerous spokes, this Papaver orientalis poppy surprises the observer with its intricate shape.

695 • The anthers of a fire-red dahlia.

The petals of a sunflower in full bloom.

Because of their complexity and bizarre shapes, the reproductive apparatus of flowers (left a passion flower and right a tulip) bring to mind alien worlds.

The reproductive apparatus of *Hemerocallis*, left, and *Sempervivum grandiflorum*, right.

702 • The sinuous shape of a just blooming dark red calla lily.

703 • A "beauty which can be seen from afar" is the meaning of the scientific name of the Waratah anemone *(Telopea speciosissima)*.

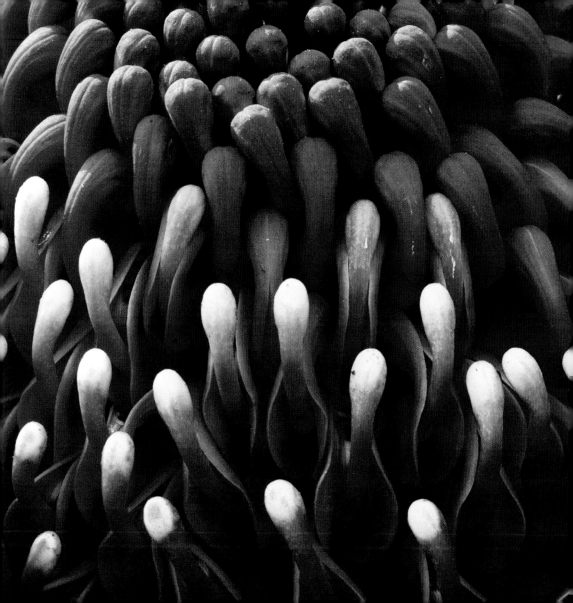

704 • The small, arrow-shaped petals of a red dahlia.

705 • The blood-red interior of an orchid, the most sensual of flowers.

● An abstract painting
in pink: like clouds,
flowers invite observers
to interpret their
shapes.

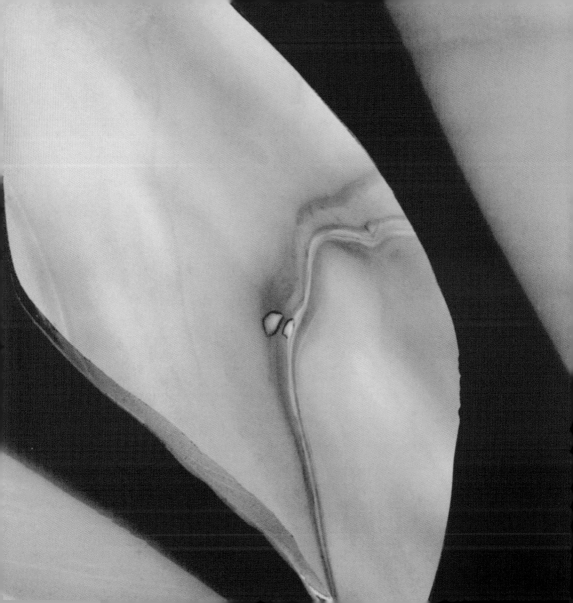

708 ● This Amazonia flower
look like a fireworks display.

708-709 ● Maui Protea
in the Hawaiian Islands.

710 • The curly pistil of an *Anthurium*.

711 • The jagged edges of a carnation corolla.

712-713 • The delicate petals of a subtly-shaded hortensia bloom .

714 • An intensely colored *Gazania*.

715 • The calyx and corolla of a hibiscus flower seen from below.

716 ● The characteristic weaves of Tillandsia flowers.

717 ● The heart of a rose.

The very recognizable corolla of a dahlia.

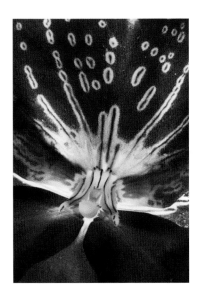

720 and 721 ● The inside of a corolla of a dappled orchid (left) and Thai vanda orchid (right).

722-723 ● Bushes of lavender: even though individual lavender flowers aren't very striking, the color of lavender bushes can be seen from miles away.

724 • The reproductive apparatus of this pansy makes its color brighter like a light in the dark.

725 • A lily opening its petals. This flower is the symbol of purity and chastity.

726 • The corolla of a tulip looks impenetrable before blooming but when
its petals open, they reveal a very delicate pistil.

727 • An anemone opens its petals in the wind which it might have been named for.

AUTHOR Biographies INDEX

▦ VALERIA MANFERTO DE FABIANIS

Valeria Manferto De Fabianis was born in Vercelli, Italy and studied arts at the Università Cattolica del Sacro Cuore in Milan, graduating with a degree in philosophy.

She is an enthusiastic traveler and nature lover. She has collaborated on the production of television documentaries and articles for the most prestigious Italian specialty magazines and has also written many photography books.

She co-founded Edizioni White Star in 1984 with Marcello Bertinetti and is the editor-in-chief.

▦ OVIDIO GUAITA

Journalist by profession and photographer by vocation, he has taught digital photography at the Academy of Fine Arts, Florence. He has published more than 30 photographic books about villas and gardens, with editions in London, Paris, New York and Tokyo. He has had various one-man photographic exhibits two of which in the Islamic Arts Museum Malaysia of Kuala Lumpur. He is president of the Tuscany delegation of the CIGV (International World Travelers Club), and since 2006 has been editor of the web magazine, *Resorts*.

PHOTO CREDITS

PHOTO CREDITS

Pages 310-311, 312, 313, 314 and 315 Warren Photographic
Page 316 Christof Wermter/zefa/Corbis
Page 317 Visuals Unlimited/Corbis
Pages 318-319 Warren Photographic
Page 319 Fritz Rauschenbach/zefa/Corbis
Pages 320, 320-321, 322 and 323 Warren Photographic
Page 324 N. A. Callow/NHPA/Photoshot
Page 325 Volkmar Brockhaus/zefa/Corbis
Pages 326 and 327 Warren Photographic
Page 328 Steve Hopkin/Ardea
Page 329 Gavriel Jecan/Corbis
Pages 330 and 331 Steve Hopkin/Ardea
Page 332 Craig Tuttle/Corbis
Page 333 Paul Freytag/zefa/Corbis
Pages 334-335 Fritz Rauschenbach/zefa/Corbis
Pages 336-337 Herbert Zettl/zefa/Corbis
Page 337 Royalty-Free/Corbis
Pages 338 and 339 James Carmichael Jr./NHPA/Photoshot
Pages 340-341 Renato Fano and Anna Flagiello
Page 342 David A. Northcott/Corbis
Page 343 Kevin Schafer
Pages 344-345 Royalty-Free/Corbis
Pages 346-347 Gary W. Carter/Corbis
Page 348 George D. Lepp/Corbis
Page 349 James Carmichael Jr./NHPA/Photoshot
Page 350 Royalty-Free/Corbis
Page 351 James Carmichael Jr./NHPA/Photoshot
Pages 352-353 T. Kitchin & V. Hurst/NHPA/Photoshot
Page 354 Kennan Ward/Corbis
Page 355 David A. Northcott/Corbis
Page 356 Michael & Patricia Fogden/Corbis
Page 357 Phil Savoie/Naturepl.com/Contrasto
Page 358 Alfredo Maiquez/Lonely Planet Images

Page 359 Kevin Schafer
Page 360 Pavel German/Auscape
Page 361 Gavriel Jecan/Corbis
Page 362 Kevin Schafer/Corbis
Page 363 Joe McDonald/Corbis
Page 364 Kevin Schafer
Page 365 Mark Bowler/NHPA/Photoshot
Pages 366-367 Charles Mauzy/Corbis
Page 369 Royalty-Free/Corbis
Page 371 Peter Smither/Corbis
Page 375 Neil Beer/Corbis
Pages 376-377 Michelle Garrett/Corbis
Pages 378-379, 380-381, 382, 383, 384-385, 386 and 387 Clay Perry/Corbis
Pages 388-389 Royalty-Free/Corbis
Page 389 Michelle Garrett/Corbis
Page 390 Clay Perry/Corbis
Pages 390-391 Michelle Garrett/Corbis
Page 392 Tania Midgley/Corbis
Pages 392-393 and 394-395 Clay Perry/Corbis
Page 395 Royalty-Free/Corbis
Pages 396, 397, 398, 399, 400-401, 402-403, 404 and 405 Clay Perry/Corbis
Pages 406-407 Frank Krahmer/zefa/Corbis
Pages 408 and 409 Clay Perry/Corbis
Pages 410-411 Dency Kane/zefa/Corbis
Page 412 Lester Lefkowitz/Corbis
Page 413 Ton Kinsbergen/Beateworks/Corbis
Pages 414, 415, 416, 417 and 418-419 Clay Perry/Corbis
Pages 420-421 Royalty-Free/Corbis
Page 421 Marco Cristofori/Corbis
Pages 422-423 Robert Holmes/Corbis
Page 423 Philip Gould/Corbis
Pages 424 and 425 Royalty-Free/Corbis
Page 426 Sylvain Grandadam/Agefotostock/Marka
Pages 426-427 and 428 Clay Perry/Corbis

Pages 428-429 Michael Boys/Corbis
Pages 430-431 Royalty-Free/Corbis
Page 431 Clay Perry/Corbis
Page 432 Earni Janes/NHPA/Photoshot
Page 433 Stephen Dalton/NHPA/Photoshot
Pages 434-435 Stefan Damm/Sime/Sie
Page 436 Greger Norrevik/Agefotostock/Marka
Page 437 Miles Ertman/Masterfile/Sie
Page 438 Royalty-Free/Corbis
Page 439 Michael Busselle/Corbis
Pages 440 and 441 Clay Perry/Corbis
Pages 442-443 Owen Franken/Corbis
Page 444 John Fairhall/Auscape
Page 445 John Beedle/Garden Picture Library
Page 446 John Pitcher/Agefotostock/Marka
Pages 447 and 448 Royalty-Free/Corbis
Pages 448-449 Lee Snider/Photo Images/Corbis
Page 450 Mark Bolton/Corbis
Page 451 Roberto Della Vite
Pages 452-453 Barbara Van Zanten/Lonely Planet Images
Page 453 Stevw Dunwell/Agefotostock/Marka
Pages 454 and 454-455 John Pitcher/Agefotostock/Marka
Pages 456-457 John and Lisa Merrill/Corbis
Page 458 Geoff Bryant/NHPA/Photoshot
Page 459 Earni Janes/NHPA/Photoshot
Pages 460-461 Michael Boys/Corbis
Page 461 Richard Cummins/Corbis
Page 462 Macduff Everton/Corbis
Pages 462-463 Martin Siepmann/Agefotostock/Marka
Pages 464-465 Shaffer/Smith Photogr/Agefotostock/Marka
Pages 466-467 Clay Perry/Corbis
Page 467 Royalty-Free/Corbis
Pages 468-469 Reinhard Schmid/Sime/Sie

PHOTO CREDITS

Page 610 Oliver Stewe/Lonely Planet Images

Page 611 Paul Panayiotou/4Corners/Sime/Sie

Pages 612-613 Jeremy Woodhouse/Masterfile/Sie

Page 613 Jonathan Smith/Lonely Planet Images

Page 614 Giovanni Simeone/Sime/Sie

Page 615 Johanna Huber/Sime/Sie

Pages 616-617 and 617 Robert Holmes/Corbis

Pages 618-619 Laurance Delderfield/Agefotostock/Marka

Pages 620-621 Gail Mooney/Corbis

Page 621 Chris Liesle/Corbis

Page 622 Owen Franken/Corbis

Pages 622-623 Roberto Rinaldi/Sime/Sie

Pages 624-625 Vince Streano/Corbis

Page 625 Jan Butchofsky-Houser/Corbis

Pages 626-627 Steve Vidler/AISA

Pages 628-629 and 630-631 Han Hartzuiker/Agefotostock/Marka

Page 632 Wolfgang Kaehler/Corbis

Page 633 Günter Gräfenhain/Sime/Sie

Pages 634-635 Douglas Peebles/Corbis

Page 635 Morton Beebe/Corbis

Pages 636 and 636-637 Richard Cummins/Corbis

Pages 638-639 Carl & Ann Purcell/Corbis

Page 639 Morton Beebe/Corbis

Pages 640-641 Jeremy Horner/Corbis

Page 642 Galen Rowell/Corbis

Page 643 Anna Clopet/Corbis

Pages 644-645 Richard Bickel/Corbis

Page 646 Pablo Corral V/Corbis

Page 647 Eric L. Wheater/Lonely Planet Images

Page 649 Royalty-Free/Corbis

Page 655 Jutta Klee/Corbis

Page 656, 657 and 658 Bloemenburo Holland/Agefotostock/Marka

Page 659 Berndt-Joel Gunnarsso/Agefotostock/Marka

Page 660 Eduard van Koolwijk/Agefotostock/Marka

Page 661 Rino Burgio/Agefotostock/Marka

Page 662 Robert Levin/Corbis

Page 663 David Young/Agefotostock/Marka

Page 664 Bloemenburo Holland/Agefotostock/Marka

Page 665 Ulrike Schneiders/Agefotostock/Marka

Pages 666, 667 and 668 Royalty-Free/Corbis

Page 669 Botanica/Garden Picture Library

Page 670 Di Lewis; Elizabeth Whiting & Associates/Corbis

Page 671 Envision/Corbis

Page 672 Royalty-Free/Corbis

Page 673 Envision/Corbis

Pages 674-675 Danilo Donadoni/Agefotostock/Marka

Page 677 Olimpo Fantuz/Sime/Sie

Page 681 S. Gallotti/Panda Photo

Pages 682-683 Vitantonio.Dell'Orto

Pages 684-685 Maurizio Biancarelli

Page 686 James Guilliam/Garden Picture Library

Page 687 Ruth Brown/Garden Picture Library

Page 688 Mark Bolton/Corbis

Page 689 Anne Hyde/Garden Picture Library

Pages 690-691 John McAnulty/Corbis

Page 691 Stephen Dalton/NHPA/Photoshot

Pages 692-693 Jean Carter/Agefotostock/Marka

Page 694 Stephen Shepard/Garden Picture Library

Page 695 Tony Howell/Garden Picture Library

Pages 696-697 Will Giles/Garden Picture Library

Page 698 Andy Small/Corbis

Page 699 David Roseburg/Corbis

Page 700 Kevin Schafer

Page 701 Vaughan Flemming/Garden Picture Library

Page 702 Royalty-Free/Corbis

Page 703 Clay Perry/Corbis

Page 704 Philip James Corwin/Corbis

Page 705 Ioannis Schinezos

Pages 706-707 Royalty-Free/Corbis

Page 708 Pete Oxford/Naturepl.com/Contrasto

Pages 708-709 Darrel Gulin/Corbis

Page 710 Ioannis Schinezos

Page 711 Royalty-Free/Corbis

Pages 712-713 William Manning/Corbis

Page 714 Richard Cummins/Corbis

Page 715 Bonnie Muench/Corbis

Page 716 Ralph A. Clevenger/Corbis

Page 717 Darrel Gulin/Corbis

Pages 718-719 John McAnulty/Corbis

Page 720 Susan Rosenthal/Corbis

Page 721 Kevin Schafer

Pages 722-723 Renato Fano and Anna Flagiello

Page 724 Theo Allofs/zefa/Corbis

Page 725 Scot Frei/Corbis

Page 726 George L. Deep/Corbis

Page 727 Steven Knights/Garden Picture Library

Page 736 Antonio Attini/Archivio White Star

Cover: Charles Mauzy/Corbis

Back cover: John Scheiber/Corbis

○ Lavender and corn poppies make one of nature's prettiest pictures.

Cover ○ A treefrog is stationed among the petals of a dahlia while awaiting an insect to capture in flight or a ground invertebrate.

Back cover ○ A purple expanse of lupine thriving in sunny, siliceous soil.